about documentary:

ANTHROPOLOGY ON FILM

A philosophy of people and art

by Robert Edmonds

Preface by Lewis Jacobs

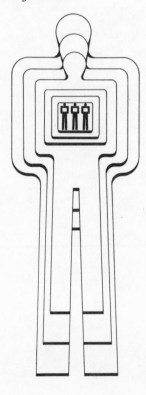

Pflaum Publishing, Dayton, Ohio

Acknowledgement is hereby gratefully made to the authors whose papers appear in this book. At a meeting after a class session they, with a number of their fellows, generously granted permission for the use of their work. Not all of those who gave this permission are represented here. Those whose papers could not be included, for one reason or another, are: Larry Buckman, Kevin Kelly, Larry Hovde, James Litwin, John Phalen and Douglas Van Doren. Mr. Van Doren's research, however, is particularly noted for having been useful in pointing me in certain directions.

A portion of Chapter II, entitled TRUTH vs. VERACITY, appeared in the November, 1971, issue of SEE, and is reprinted with the kind permission of the co-publishers of that journal, Screen Educators' Society of Chicago and Film Education Resources Corporation of Northfield, Illinois.

My particular gratitude is to be expressed to Jean Savelle who typed the whole manuscript with extraordinary accuracy, celerity and cheerfulness.

It is not possible adequately to thank my wife without whose constant interest and encouragement, perceptive insights and sensitive responses I could accomplish little. For me, without Shirley nothing really happens.

Paper cover ISBN   0•8278•0294•3

Cloth cover ISBN   0•8278•0295•1

Library of Congress Catalog Card Number 74•84292

TABLE OF CONTENTS

John Grierson, more than anyone else, stimulated the growth of documentary film-making and documentary film-viewing around the world, and generated those benign environments in which so many documentarians, myself included, could learn and practise our arts. This book is dedicated to him.

PREFACE

by Lewis Jacobs

How refreshing it is to come upon a new book about documentary that doesn't present yet another interpretation or evaluation of Nanook! In fact, nowhere in it will you find attention given to the interpretation or evaluation of any individual documentary film. Not only is this refreshing, because by now we have perhaps had enough of this kind of analysis and exegesis, but it is precisely for what it contains in place of these that considerable value is to be found in Robert Edmonds' new book. It is a book that lives up to its name. It is indeed *About Documentary*—documentary film as a social statement, a social and personal artistic endeavor, an attitude of film-maker, audience and teacher. Perhaps most important of all, the book demonstrates that students, not less than teachers, can have something important to say when they are given the opportunity of doing so.

It is something less than half a century ago that John Grierson first coined the phrase "documentary film." For more than two-thirds of that time Edmonds has been actively engaged in making and teaching films. In the early summer of 1941 he became one of the young members of the then very new National Film Board of Canada headed by John Grierson. It was here that his own education in film began. When he first joined the National

Film Board, he says, he "didn't know film was a clear substance with emulsion on one side of it." Ten years later he had met and learned about film from a considerable number of important documentary film-makers and he had himself made a number of films that had gained international awards.

Edmonds has always been deeply committed to teaching. I have visited his classes at Columbia College in Chicago and we have been colleagues in summer institutes of related arts in Pennsylvania. For many years he taught as an avocation while continuing to make films. He began full-time teaching when he became Chairman of the Motion Picture Department of Columbia College in 1967. His teaching of the various crafts—editing, cinematography, writing and so on—was generated and enriched by his personal film-making activity, and yet he has told me that he first began to teach many years ago for what he considers a somewhat egocentric reason. He found that this was an invaluable way to find out just what he had learned about film, for, when one has to articulate for others what one has learned empirically (and this was the only avenue of learning film open to those of us who began to make films in those days), one must undertake what surely is the basic educational task: the task of asking WHY? Why do I do this and not that in such-and-such a circumstance? Why do I think this and not that about such-and-such a way of doing things or about such-and-such a statement?

As a film-maker/teacher for many years myself, I have learned how important this is. In order to teach, in order to organize and articulate for our students all those things which we have learned empirically, we must conceptualize our experience and knowledge. In order for the student to understand all of his experiences and learnings, he, too, must learn to conceptualize. Herein lies the importance of the present book, for Edmonds demonstrates through those student papers collected here how he has been able to direct the attention of the members of his class to this fundamental process. The term-paper subjects generated by the class and the papers responding to those subjects demonstrate the importance of this process of conceptualization. They demonstrate its value to the students because of the creative involvement of the students in the process itself, an involvement that seems to be lacking in those term-papers and examinations that are focused on the regurgitation of data and interpretations already laid down. But the process also has immense value to the teacher because from the papers delivered to him he can far better judge not how well his students can recite but the degree to which they have developed emotional and intellectual responsiveness. This is not to say that all, or perhaps even any, of the papers written by the students are earth-shaking in the importance or originality of their material or approach (nor is it to say that these qualities are in any way lacking!), but they do demonstrate the clear value to the students of helping them learn to conceptualize, and the immensely enriching "feedback" provided to the teacher on the basis of which he can develop his teaching and his courses in new directions and on new levels. In his own chapters, Edmonds has approached some basic concepts in ways that seem new and valuable and illustrate the kind of thinking that generates the stimulus and environment for the work of his students.

The message of the book is one which I hope will be received by all those who want to learn or teach about documentary films, for it can only generate many new and helpful ideas.

INTRODUCTION

It is almost thirty-three years since I first joined the National Film Board of Canada and was introduced to documentary films. My background had been humanistic and this seems to have made my encounter with documentary films and documentarians most congenial. I had had the good luck of having exciting intellectual friends, and one of these was a brilliant research surgeon and Professor of Experimental Surgery, Dr. Jacob Markowitz. He was not only a scientific researcher, but a very serious litterateur, and he was for many years the publisher of the *Canadian Poetry Magazine*. He was also a relative by marriage and we met often. While I was still in high school he gave me two instructions that were then novel to me, but which have remained leading influences in my life. They both dealt with the importance of asking questions. On one occasion I had remarked to him, "You know, Marko, it must be wonderful to be able to make all those discoveries and find out all those new things." To which he replied, "No. Finding out the new things isn't really very difficult. Usually the discoveries can be made by any well-trained technician. The basis of good scientific research lies in asking the right questions. From these the technician can make the discoveries."

On another occasion he instructed me concerning the right

way to read a book—a non-fiction book, of course. He told me that in most cases the author wrote in the introduction what he proposed to demonstrate in the book and how he intended to demonstrate it. In the conclusion the author would summarize what he had demonstrated in the book and recall the techniques of the demonstration. The main body of the book was taken up with the demonstration and the detail. It was therefore not necessary to read most non-fiction books: read only the introduction and the conclusion! But he gave me a most solemn *caveat.* "Never," he said, "do you, for any reason, have the obligation to agree with the author or believe him. You do have the obligation to read his work and try to find where he has made any errors; but, if you do not find the errors, you have now two further obligations: you must believe him *for now,* but you must seek more in the attempt to refute him!" He called this "having a dialogue with the author."

Notice that good reading as well as good research had, for Jacob Markowitz, the need for continued questioning. His instruction of me came early in my time in high school, just when my own intellectual activity was being energized. His instruction was sufficiently iconoclastic to appeal to an adolescent, and occasional repeated references over the succeeding years reinforced the teaching so that it became a way of thinking for me for the rest of my life. This book arises out of that kind of background, at least in part.

Among my friends and colleagues in the National Film Board were many who loved to talk and think about their work, "their art." Often we had *kaffeeklatsches* during which we explored, each in his own way, the meaning of documentary to him. It may be an astonishing observation, but whenever documentary film-makers gather together the talk gets around to film, theory, the relationships of films to society, or of film-makers to society, for at least a portion of the evening. The subjects are nothing if not profound, even if the remarks that are made are somewhat superficial! Documentarists, you see, are also verbal people. They talk a lot about documentary. For me at least this meant that I was led to think a lot about it, too. And to ask questions about it.

As time went by and circumstances developed, I met some exciting people in the documentary "movement." In conversations with these people sparks were struck for me that lit new roads of thought. Later, during my teaching, further lights were lit. Out of all this emerge some of the ideas that appear in this book, ideas generated by dialogue with other film-makers, with friends of all kinds, and with students. Since I don't stop talking, I suppose I shall continue to enjoy meeting and speaking with all kinds of people for a long time to come. If this happens, as I hope it will, I shall have the opportunity of learning a great deal more. That may change some or much of what I have said in this book, for I hope that I will always be open to change. Not changing is not growing. Not growing is dying.

Because of the instruction I have reported above, I hope that you will read the book and have a dialogue with me—even though tacitly—and let us extend that hope that in those areas in which you find I have made errors you will be able to instruct me. In any case, since I now know the pitfalls of disclosing in the introduction what I hope to say in the body of the book, I will refrain from saying anything more.

It may bother you a little to find that I have said the same thing more than once in the book, although perhaps in different context. My philosophy is not linear. My perception of the world is that all things relate to all things, and, by so doing, may develop more than one meaning for me. No relationship is a one-way street. That which affects is itself affected. I find that, just as in art so in all other things in life, ambivalences and ambiguities carry for me more meaning, more truth. Our educational system doesn't help our students understand this. The square root of 4 is expressed as being "plus 2 or minus 2," when, in fact, it should be "plus 2 *and* minus 2." If we learn nothing more of Einstein's plastic thinking, we should learn that things can be observed in more than one way simultaneously. The world is contrapuntal. Ambiguity and contradiction have deep meaning and deep consequences. It is from them that our most productive inquiries arise. But it is from this kind of thinking that I am led to repeat, on occasion, certain statements because they occur in different context or different circumstances. I can only ask that, instead of becoming bored by the repetition, you attend to the context, the environment, in which you find that repetition, and the new relationships that may appear.

try as director, producer, writer,

and is the recipient of an

ward. He came to New York as

SDIG on the completion of a

task of organizing the Midwest

ild.

his new duties on Monday, August

ll be presented for membership

Meeting September 17th.

e to 600 film and television

- 30 -

try as director, producer, writer,

and is the recipient of an

ward. He came to New York as

SDIG on the completion of a

task of organizing the Midwest

ild.

his new duties on Monday, August

ll be presented for membership

Meeting September 17th.

to 600 film and television

- 30 -

CHAPTER I

Documentary: Anthropology on Film

There is a saying that is attributed, I believe, to Mark Twain, to the effect that: Everybody always *talks* about the weather but nobody ever *does* anything about it! Documentary differs in this respect: It seems that nearly everybody talks about it, at one time or another, and, from the number of films that enter such conversations, it seems that nearly everybody is making one! The problem is that there is no clear understanding of what documentary really is.

In the winter of 1932, John Grierson wrote: "Documentary is a clumsy description, but let it stand."[1] He of all people had the right to make that statement since it had been he who had first applied the term "documentary" to a film. In an unsigned review of Robert Flaherty's *Moana*, Grierson had declared that ". . . *Moana* being a visual account of events in the daily life of a Polynesian youth and his family, has documentary value."[2] No one can quibble with the use of the term documentary to describe the quality that appears *on film* of the subject material Grierson indicated. Unfortunately, from that use onward, the term appears to have suffered more than most from unending semantic slides, so that now there is a plethora of definitions as well as a plethora of films!

In television, almost any film that is not "fictional"—what-

ever that may mean—is called a documentary. Amongst users
of industrial films, a "trip through the plant" is called a documentary. Painlevé's film *The Seahorse* is said to be a documentary, the film record of the first moon landing is said to be
a documentary, and Leni Riefenstahl's *Triumph of the Will* is
said to be a documentary. Are they all documentaries? Are any
of them documentaries? Just what is a documentary? Is it important to define documentary in the first place?

The need for definition is built into the whole language
process. Language is the means people use for communicating
one with another (even though it can on occasion be used for
the purpose of obfuscating or preventing communication). If it
is the means of communicating, or even if it is the means of
hiding communication, it can only work effectively if both
transmittor and receptor of the communication agree on the
meaning of the terms in which the transmission is couched.
Thus it is that the meaning of each of the terms of a communication, and the meanings of the collections of terms, exist because of mutual convention arrived at by the parties to the
communication. This meaning-arrived-at-by-convention is in
fact the definition of the term or the phrase. In order that the
possibility of error in understanding the meaning of the communication be reduced as much as possible, the definition
becomes more and more refined. Each area of specialization, for
example, develops its own special language or jargon in order
to provide terms with specially refined definitions for use by the
specialists. Those of us in the general public find sufficient discomfort in the general term "cancer" but physicians and re-
searchers need more specific terms such as "carcinoma," "sar-
coma" and "melanoma," for example.

If we are to talk about certain films, it becomes highly desirable to agree on the language we use. Instead of continually
saying "films like . . ." and then listing five or a dozen or a
hundred films that appear to bear those characteristics com-
monly shared that make them a category for us who are
communicating, it is clearly more desirable to agree on a word
or a phrase that indicates "the films that exhibit such-and-such
characteristics." If the word we seek to use in such circumstances is "documentary" then what we are seeking to agree on
is the collection of characteristics exhibited by those films which
we will understand to be just included in our category.

Our experience in this world is phenomenological, that is to say, our awareness of our environment, immediate or extended, is developed only through our perceptions of our confrontations with the things and their relationships in that environment. We become aware of those things and relationships by discovering differences between them. After a number of similar experiences we draw general ideas about those experiences and we then develop a word to represent those general ideas. Each word is a something that stands for a generally observed set of attributes. Each word (or phrase) is itself, therefore, a conceptualization, that is to say, each word or phrase stands for an idea, a conceptualization, of the collection of attributes.

The smaller the group of attributes and the more clearly perceived they have been, the more specific is the meaning of the word that represents them. The larger the number of attributes, the less clearly they have been perceived and conceptualized, the less clear is the meaning of the word employed. Lack of clarity in the use of words obviously leads to lack of clarity of statement and, reflexively, leads to lack of clarity in thinking on the part of the person using those words. The reason for this is simple. If the clarity of meaning of a word is dependent upon the clarity of perception and conceptualization of the ideas that word is to communicate, then it follows that if the word is unclearly used it represents unclear perception and conceptualization which, in turn, generate further lack of clarity. Since the clarity of our perceptions is a major way for us to define ourselves, to find our own individual identities, it is incumbent upon us to try to be as clear as possible in our thinking. It is for these reasons that it is important to seek clarity of definition and clarity of word use.

Unfortunately, it appears to be a foible of some cultures, especially apparent in America, to permit a word to develop functions in addition to that of describing a thing or an idea. Words do indeed begin their careers by bearing conventionally agreed upon meanings descriptive of things or ideas. But, since words are generalizations, they function as names of categories, because each generalization is, in fact, a category in which the collection of attributes identified by the word are found. Perhaps because of habits of thought growing out of millennia of Platonic thinking, perhaps for any of a hundred other reasons, the *idea* of each category becomes fixed. The idea, and the word representing it, become a Procrustean bed. Every phonomenon which confronts us must, in order to fit into our preconceived notion of things, fit into such and such a category. Worse, the categories themselves begin to be normative. Forcing the *idea* of the new phenomenon which confronts us into a Procrustean bed becomes a normative process that directs the form of our thinking.

This process is not greatly dissimilar to what happens to us when our thinking is distorted by a neurosis or, worse, a psychosis. With these disabilities, we are subjected to patterned responses. Because of some image-making pattern developed in us in childhood, we translate each experience into forms of those pattern images. Our reactions are to the pattern and not to the phenomenon or the experience. For example, father, doctor, teacher, policeman and probably a host of other people may all be "authority figures" and, with neurotic or psychotic disabilities, we respond to the authority figure and not to the father, doctor, teacher, policeman as individuals who confront us in their individual circumstances. Our thinking is patterned because of some psychic disturbance.

In the same way, when we use words as labels, that is, when we use them as normative Procrustean beds, they, too, become directive of our thinking.

There is only one approach to curing ourselves. We must continue to ask questions. We must continue to question ourselves about the words we use, and the meanings of those words, and the reality of our perceptions, and the way in which the words we use reflect our perceptions. This admonition to continuous questioning will be found repeated throughout this book. It is repeated without apology; on the contrary, be assured that the repetition is intentional. If I have learned only one thing in my life it is that I must always ask questions *of myself* about everything I *have learned* and everything *new*, as I learn.

The process of learning, as differentiated from the process by which one achieves training, is the process of questioning. The questions must be developed by the learner. It is "training" if all he does is to respond to some questioner other than himself. His answers are not thought of by himself because he does not develop any means of evaluating his own answers in terms of his own experience and perceptions. Instead, to answer the questions of others is simply to demonstrate the power of recitation or regurgitation. Never forget that regurgitation invariably indicates lack of complete digestion! If one learns that questions are much more important than answers, one continues to grow.

It is now time to question the almost myriad definitions of documentary film. Grierson, who first used the word documentary as we have described, said it was clumsy. He later attempted to define his definition, and he is quoted by Paul Rotha as saying that documentary means "the creative treatment of actuality."[3] Since there is certainly no uniformity in the perception of actuality, and since there is a limitless variety of ways in which creativity may modify "actuality," Grierson's definition is, indeed, somewhat clumsy. Moreover, it gets itself involved with a kind of qualitative or normative process when it employs the word "creative." Others who write about documentary films, talk about them, and even make them, have developed some qualms about defining what they are talking about or making. Lindsay Anderson has said: ". . . one of the things that has fouled up the discussion of documentaries, I think, in recent years has been the identification of documentary with information or even instruction. Maybe it's a word that has outlived its usefulness, because I think that it no longer has a very clear significance."[4] In passing, it should be noted that Anderson quotes Grierson differently from Rotha. For Anderson, Grierson defined documentary as "the creative *interpretation* of actuality"[5] (the emphasis is mine). Is the difference significant?

Basil Wright, another British documentarian and colleague of Grierson, also quotes him, using the words remembered by Lindsay Anderson, and at the same time exhibits the same attitude of advocacy that underlies all of Grierson's work. He says: "The function of documentary is not merely education, but also revelation."[6] Grierson was less delicate. For him the need to reveal was the road to vigorous advocacy. "If we are to persuade, we have to reveal, and we have to reveal in terms of reality."[7] But note here a slight change that is in truth gargantuan. The word "actuality" has been replaced by "reality." This change is of basic importance, in my view, as will be seen in later chapters.

Perhaps Henri Storck, in an oblique way, has put his finger on the underlying problem in Grierson's definition of documentary. For Storck "Grierson always, how shall I say it, saw documentary forms as a weapon, as a tool for creating a society. He thought film should deal with problems of information and even propaganda, in the service of the general public. That is, he didn't see documentary film as a form in itself, a category of film."[8]

Georges Franju is much more outspoken than Grierson in putting forth the view that documentary is an agitational form of cinema. "Documentary is to the cinema what the poster is to painting. A poster has a clear, precise question to resolve, which is why there are really good posters."[9] This last sentence also includes, obviously, a criterion. If a clear, precise question makes possible a really good poster, then a documentary that addresses itself to a clear, precise question has found the possibility of being a really good documentary! One might observe, as an obiter dictum, that perhaps clarity is the mark of any good work, indeed a necessary attribute of all good works.

On the other end of the scale, Richard Cawston prefers to make the "totally objective type of program"—a possibility that we shall be discussing later. He says, "I think there is at one end of the scale the totally objective type of program, which is what I have made more of myself; at the other end of the scale there is the fully subjective committed documentary which is made by a man who wants to use it to say something himself."[10] The background for Cawston's apparent preference for "totally objective" films—and he has made a great number of films over a number of years at BBC—is implied in something else that he has said about documentary. "Its job is to reflect society, not to influence it, but in reflecting society accurately, one tries to reflect, as it were, the spearheads of society. One tries to take people who are slightly ahead in their thinking, communicate their thoughts to the masses, which enables those who are a little lagging behind to catch up with the ones in front. And in that way, of course, it must help to change society."[11] The words that Cawston has used to enlarge upon the desirability of dispassion disclose an Olympian separation between himself as film-maker-teacher and his audience. It appears to me that this is a fundamental and dangerous alienation for any communicator or artwork-maker, especially since Cawston's words exhibit not compassion but condescension, a sense of "them" and "us" instead of "we."

The World Union of Documentary Film-makers issued a definition in 1948 that attempts to please every member, and succeeds in trying to sit on many chairs at the same time. "All methods of recording on celluloid any aspect of reality interpreted either by factual shooting or by sincere and justifiable reconstruction, so as to appeal either to reason or emotion, for the purpose of stimulating the desire for, and the widening of, human knowledge and understanding, and of truthfully posing problems and their solutions in the spheres of economics, culture and human relations."[12] There are so many hedges in this definition that it does, in fact, serve little purpose. The only aspect of it that one can grasp and hold on to is in the last phrase: ". . . truthfully posing problems and their solutions in the spheres of economics, culture, and human relations."

It appears that there is probably more agreement concerning these social aspects of documentary film. Lindsay Anderson, for example, admits that "documentary is certainly a form, I think, that stresses the social relationships . . ."[13] On another occasion, Grierson was more specific. He said, "You photograph the natural life, but you also, by your juxtaposition of detail, create an interpretation of life."[14] In 1936, Paul Rotha wrote: "The documentary method, as a distinct kind of film, as an interpretation of social feeling and philosophic thought quite different in purpose and form from the entertainment motives of story film, has materialised largely as the result of sociological, political and educational requirements."[15] "Surely, it is pointless, if not impossible, to bring alive the realities of the modern world unless we do so in such a manner as to base our themes on the relationship of Man to the world in which he lives?"[16] Thirty-seven years later, in a class he conducted in Paris, I heard Jean Rouch say, "Documentary is current history because it deals with how people live, what they want, how they try to get it." As Lewis Jacobs has written, "The documentary film came to be identifiable as a special kind of picture with a clear social purpose . . ."[17] This much of his sentence concerns the content of documentary. The remainder of his sentence deals, as do so many of the definitions, not with what documentary is about, but rather with the style in which it may be made. ". . . dealing with real people and real events, as opposed to staged scenes of imaginary characters and fictional stories of the studio-made pictures."[18]

We said earlier that it becomes necessary to be clear in how we think, clear in the use of words that represent what we think. It does not appear useful to me for the meaning of the word documentary to deal both with the content of documentary films and the style with which that content is presented.

It is because that confusion has occurred over such a long period that the World Union of Documentary Film-makers finally produced a definition that is really gobble-de-gook, and Lindsay Anderson throws up his hands and says, "Maybe it's a word that has outlived its usefulness, because I think that it no longer has a very clear significance." If we disentangle the two *kinds* of meanings that have attached to documentary, that is to say, if we disentangle the *material* of documentary (i.e., subject matter) from the *manner* of its presentation, we can deal with each kind of meaning separately. This will provide us with greater clarity because we can more nearly arrive at universal agreement (the convention by which the meaning of the word can be transmitted from one person to another).

Let us agree that the word documentary denotes a kind of film that presents, in some manner or another, reality or actuality (whatever *they* may mean). But, unless that reality or actuality relates in a clear way to humans, how do we recognize the meaningfulness of reality or actuality? We have already quoted Paul Rotha: "Surely it is pointless, if not impossible, to bring alive the realities of the modern world unless we do so in such a manner as to base our themes on the relationship of Man to the world in which he lives?" Consider: the relationship of man to the world in which he lives; or Rouch's "how people live, what they want and how they try to get it"; or the World Union's "problems and their solutions in the spheres of economics, culture and human relations." These points of agreement provide us with the definition of documentary film. Documentary is simply anthropology on film! Let us repeat, DOCUMENTARY IS ANTHROPOLOGY ON FILM.

This use of the word documentary is not normative. There is no implication of *how* a documentary is to be made, what attitudes the documentarist should possess, nor of the philosophy which invests the film. These qualities of meaning are purposely stripped from the meaning that is to be found in the word documentary, because those qualities are too important to be included. They should be dealt with on their own. Social attitude, philosophy, aesthetics are indeed the normative bases which provide criteria for judging whether the documentary film is a *good* documentary film or not, and we shall be addressing our attention to those very qualities later. For now, however, let it suffice that our definition of documentary is "Anthropology on film."

With this definition, there can be no confusion as to whether a sales training film is a documentary film, or whether within the term documentary can be included travelogues, lecture films, didactic films, editorial films, scientific records or a host of other varieties. We must, therefore, in a documentary seek only for anthropology, for the reality, the actuality, of man's relationship to his work, his environment and his society.

But—what *is* reality? What *is* actuality? Is there some way for us to find out?

[1] *Grierson on Documentary*, Forsyth Hardy, Harcourt, Brace and Company, New York, 1947, p. 99.
[2] *The Documentary Tradition*, Lewis Jacobs, Hopkinson and Blake, New York, 1971, p. 25.
[3] *Documentary Film*, Paul Rotha, Faber and Faber Limited, London, 1936, p. 68.
[4] *Documentary Explorations*, G. Roy Levin, Doubleday & Company, Garden City, 1971, p. 62.
[5] *Ibid*.
[6] *World Documentary*, Basil Wright. Documentary '48, Edinburgh, 1948.
[7] *Op. cit.*, Forsyth Hardy, p. 265.
[8] *Op. cit.*, G. Roy Levin, p. 156.
[9] *Ibid.*, p. 120.
[10] *Op. cit.*, G. Roy Levin, p. 87.
[11] *Ibid.*, p. 94.
[12] *Op. cit.*, Basil Wright. Also quoted by Cavalcanti, Chicago, May, 1973.
[13] *Op. cit.*, G. Roy Levin, p. 63.
[14] *Op. cit.*, Forsyth Hardy, p. 103.
[15] *Op. cit.*, Paul Rotha, p. 115.
[16] *Ibid.*, p. 124.
[17] *Op. cit.*, Lewis Jacobs, p. 2.
[18] *Op. cit.*, Lewis Jacobs, p. 2.

CHAPTER II

Truth vs. Veracity

Truth may be stranger than fiction, but veracity can be stranger than truth.

In the entertainment and trade paper, *Variety* (February 16, 1966), the following paragraph introduced a news story.

> *"Narrow-gauge (16mm) film has been chosen by both the political right and left as the primary weapon in the continuing struggle to gain supporters in the intensifying debate over U.S. involvement in Vietnam. Fulton Lewis 3d's "While Brave Men Die," is the 'rightwing' entry on the screen battleground, and the latest 'leftwing' entry is a projected hour-long picture as yet untitled, to be made within the next four months by tyro film-makers Peter Gessner and Robert Kramer. (First is son of NYU's Professor of Cinema, Robert Gessner.)"*

The story went on to say:

> *"Aimed at 'those who have been able to remain indifferent to the issue of U.S. involvement in Vietnam,' the Gessner-Kramer film would attempt to treat not only the war, but the U.S. debate over the war and 'raise crucial questions,' Gessner said. Though admittedly not 'impartial,' the film would not be 'blatant propaganda,' expressing the 'ideological platitudes, hyperboles and slogans' of the films now in use by the left.*

> *"Currently researching sources for newsreel footage from*

*the news services, networks, foreign news services, and North
and South Vietnamese sources, Gessner claims he learned of
the Lewis film because everywhere he inquired, film librar-
ians would mention that Lewis had already been there."*

Peter Gessner finds that "while researching sources for newsreel footage from the news services networks, foreign news services and North and South Vietnamese sources," Lewis has
already sought out similar scenes from the same sources. The
same newsreel footage, pictures of things which actually happened, can, it appears, be used to express opposite interpretations of the same events. This phenomenon makes it incumbent
upon all of us who look at films to recognize what it is in the
film medium that permits such a paradox.

Film shots, like words, take their meaning from the other
words in the sentences in which they are used. Just as a word
is neither subject nor object until it occurs in a sentence, so a
film shot is "alienated" from meaning until it is edited into a
filmic sentence. Let us suppose we had made three shots at
different times and at different places. Let us suppose that the
first shot is a close-up from a low angle of a man's head against
a blue sky as he turns to look partly to his left. We shot this
one day when we were vacationing in Florida. Our second
shot is a shot of the Capitol dome in Washington. Our third
shot is a close-up of a man's feet as they ascend some stone
steps. This last shot was made on a clear day in front of the
Art Institute in Chicago. If we edit these shots in the order in
which they have been described, it becomes quite clear that a
man sees the dome and then enters the Capitol. The scenes
were not taken in the same place. They had no unity of time,
place nor motivation until they were put together.

The cinematic time, space and motivation that become manifest in this sequence are peculiar to it, part of it, and bear no
relationship to any other kind of time, space or motivation.
Now, motivation implies action, for it is only action (or a
deliberate abstention from action, and such an abstention is
surely active) that can be motivated. In our sequence, it is clear,
there is action. A man walks, a man looks up, he sees a building
and begins to enter it. This is action. But, does action always
require movement? In his classic textbook, *Film Technique,*
V. I. Pudovkin reports an interesting experiment that he and
his instructor and co-worker, Kuleshov, made.

"We took from some film or other," he says, "several close-ups of the well-known actor Mosjukhin. We chose close-ups which were static and which did not express any feeling at all—quiet close-ups. We joined those close-ups, which were all similar, with other bits of film in three different combinations. In the first combination the close-up of Mosjukhin was immediately followed by a shot of a plate of soup standing on a table. It was obvious and certain that Mosjukhin was looking at this soup. In the second combination the face of Mosjukhin was joined to shots showing a coffin in which lay a dead woman. In the third the close-up was followed by a shot of a little girl playing with a funny toy bear. When we showed the three combinations to an audience which had not been let into the secret the result was terrific. The public raved about the acting of the artist. They pointed out the heavy pensiveness of his mood over the forgotten soup, were touched and moved by the deep sorrow with which he looked on the dead woman, and admired the light, happy smile with which he surveyed the girl at play. But we knew that in all three cases the face was exactly the same."[1]

As far as the audience was concerned, each of the three different groupings of shots associated with the face of Mosjukhin provided a different motivation, because, for the audience, he reacted differently in each case; and a reaction can only be caused by something that is the stimulus for that reaction, the motivation. But let us be clear about it. Pudovkin is very careful to state, "We chose close-ups which were static and which did not express any feeling at all . . ." There was surely no motion. Yet there was an apparent motivation. We have no choice, therefore, but to realize that action need not imply motion. Action can be internal. If you think about it for a moment, while you do so you may not move a muscle (other than the normal autonomous movements of your lungs, heart and eyelids) but you would certainly be the first to affirm that the process of thinking is an activity, an action.

However, because such internal action is, to the observer, less explicit than motional activity, it is open to a far wider range of possible interpretations. From Pudovkin's example, given a recorded image of non-action, i.e., of no movement, an almost limitless number of groups of shots can be selected to edit in company with it, and each such editing will provide its own directed interpretation.

The shots in our example of the man at the Capitol building might have been made as snapshots, or they might have been photographed intentionally. In Pudovkin's example they were, in his own statement, taken "from some film or other." The same phenomenon of motivation, and cinematic unity of time and place, occur in the sequences of Mosjukhin, because of the inherent dynamic in an edited sequence. Now, in all of the examples, we have been dealing with fictitious situations, with stories that are fictitious. What happens when we deal with newsreel footage, with "actuality" film material?

Let us suppose that we have been sent out to make a complete motion picture record of a large picnic. It has been organized by an ethnic chorus group for the members and their families. We are a film crew composed of several cameramen, a director, and crew members as needed. It is a lovely, warm day in late spring. The park in which the picnic is taking place is beautiful. The leaves are rich and green, and the late spring shrubs and flowers are in bloom. We arrive in plenty of time, in fact we are early, and we dispose our cameramen about the whole area. The families arrive, park their cars and hurry happily to the picnic site. There are to be refreshments and entertainment. Our cameras go about making footage of all the preparations and activities. We record the families arriving. We see the food tables being set up and dressed. We see the great open pit where the meat is being roasted. We take pictures of soft drinks being put on ice and of ice cream being carried to several counters. We see carvers cutting the meat for roasting. Everything is a proper subject for our cameras. There are long shots in which many people and activities are visible. We take close-ups in which, perhaps, only a hand picking up a sharp knife from a table is to be seen—the kind of shot that we intend to use later when we edit the various sequences.

The picnic progresses and everyone is having a wonderful time. Our cameras continue to grind out footage of all that goes on. At one point, during the time when the guests are approaching the tables with their food, a gang of toughs appears and attempts to break up the proceedings. The hooligans cause considerable disturbance and our cameras, still covering all that is happening, get pictures of it all. After a short time, however, everything becomes quiet again. The police, who had been called at the outbreak of the rowdiness, manage to collect the roughs and persuade them to leave. The picnic continues.

Afterwards, when we have our negative processed and printed and we screen the footage before editing it, we find that we have a very satisfactory collection of shots. There is plenty of material—long shots, medium shots, close-ups, of everything we will need. Everything was shot just as it happened. We have no gaps in our story. Our close-ups, for example, show lots of good faces, most of them happy as can be, but plenty of angry faces during the disturbance, too—individual faces, each with its own expression of anger, fear or dismay. And so we begin to edit.

While we are engaged in this—and it takes us several days because we shot so many feet of film—newspaper articles report on the picnic and the disturbance. Radio announcements, speeches on the platform and on television, newspaper editorials, make much of the appearance of the toughs and the ensuing rowdiness. Who caused the mêlée? Some of the statements support the picnickers. Others attack them. Who started the violence? Were the people giving the picnic hostile? Was the violence premeditated by the toughs? The speeches, the editorials, the news stories in all the news media take opposing views. But don't worry. We can show exactly what happened when our film is finished, because it was all shot at the place and during the time of the disturbance.

Suddenly, we find that something strange can happen with our film. Even though it was shot as a kind of newsreel, even though it is "actuality" footage, even though it is *real* and not acted, even though we photographed everything that happened just as it happened, we discover that now it has become a series of shots and these shots are subject to all of the plasticity, the versatility, and the dynamics of any other film shots. We need take only two or three of them, place them out of sequence, and, lo and behold! because of that peculiar dynamic that arises within an edited sequence permitting us to imply motivation where none existed before, we can tell a story that will make it quite clear that it was the fault of the hosts, and not of the intruders, that the violence occurred.

We can take all of our story and edit it according to a proper sequence of events up to and including the arrival of the uninvited gang. We return to show the people preparing the food. This brief sequence ends with a face looking up. We see one shot of the gang again. Now we use that one shot of the carver's hand picking up a carving knife, then a face twisted in dismay, another face exhibiting fear, a third face distorted in anger, then a series of shots of the mêlée itself. And now, who caused the violence? Why, one of the carving people at the food tables started it all, of course!

Yet we were there. We saw what occurred. The disturbance was in all truth initiated by the gang of roughnecks.

What has happened? What have we done? We have used real, actual, *true* shots to tell a violent untruth!

The real, the actual, the true shots have veracity. They were photographs of real, actual, true people in real, actual and true happenings. But, though these shots have veracity, they do not tell the truth. Our ability to create motivation in a film sequence has manifested itself in such a way that we now find a difference between veracity and truth where, in the dictionary, none exists.

This dynamic element of plasticity, cinematic motivation, can be a major problem in the making of news reportage films and films of actuality. The change from veracity and truth to veracity and untruth can be a subtle change indeed. It can even occur simply by the desire of the film-maker to impart a greater "dramatic" impact to his finished film. It often occurs "unintentionally," which is, perhaps, really to say that it occurs because of an attitude of carelessness to the distinction between veracity and truth.

The film and television industries are highly departmentalized. Each of the skill-crafts hews, to a great extent, to its own line. In the coverage of news, for example, it is a common practice for the director and cameraman to remain in the field, sending back the footage they shoot as they complete each assignment. The film then goes to the editing department where it is put together. In the absence of the director (or someone who was at the scene of the incident that has been recorded and is now performing his function for him), it is quite apparent that there may easily be a difference between the sense of the final edited form of the footage and the facts as they occurred while the camera crew took the pictures. No matter how good the intentions may be, it is almost impossible that there should be any other result. If the intentions, on the other hand, happen to be less than good, then there are plenty of ways in which the result can be a guaranteed untruth.

Translating veracity into untruth can be obvious and blatant, or it can be subtle. In either case it can be a violent contradiction of reality, a contradiction that may have arisen out of all possible malice aforethought. A few years ago, during hearings conducted in San Francisco by the House Committee on Un-American Activities, demonstrations occurred accompanied by conflicts of some violence between the police and the demonstrators. A vigorous controversy has arisen in this country concerning a film, entitled *Operation Abolition,* which dealt with this demonstration and conflict. The controversy was specifically concerned with whether the film was or was not truthful. The shots themselves had veracity.

On the other hand, on Memorial Day, 1937, pickets at the Republic Steel Company in South Chicago were fired on by the police. All controversy about this was silenced when the facts were clearly established before a Senate investigating committee by the exhibition of actuality footage presented *in the order in which it had been photographed, before editing.*[2]

Our law courts have recognized for a very long time that truth and veracity need not be identical. In how many courtroom scenes that you have watched on the stage, the screen or television—perhaps you've even appeared yourself—have you heard the clerk of the court swear in a witness with the phrase "the truth, the whole truth and nothing but the truth"? When you think about that timeworn phrase it will become clear to you that those who built our legal structure understood that there are degrees and kinds of truth. They recognized that facts, true in themselves, may be untrue if they are in the wrong context, or if they are not modified by any context at all. Thus, to ensure as best they could that the witness will provide answers of truth, *essential* truth, the oath requires the statement of not only part of the facts, but all of them; all of them, but without any embellishment of fiction.

It becomes apparent, then, that truth is not so much a matter of facts as it is a matter of relationships. If we leave out certain facts in our account of a happening, or if we re-arrange the facts, or add additional material, we cloud, and perhaps change radically, the important relationships that are the essence of truth. In our hypothetical project of filming the picnic, the individual shots are all records of facts. Each shot is a record of something that did indeed occur. However, by rearranging those records of facts, those shots, we can construct a story in which there is no essential truth.

It is because truth is really a matter of relationships that we can produce good fiction in prose and poetry, on the stage and on the screen. Good fiction is that in which the relationships between the people, and between the people and their environment, contain the essence of truth. And now another paradox appears. Truth, essential truth, can occur without the presence of any "facts"! In a novel, a play, or in a motion picture, we can create a complete population, we can re-enact every scene, we can invent the locale and the incidents—thus there is no "actuality," no fact at all—yet, if the relationships between the people we have created, and between those people and their environment, are true, we have created a work of fiction that exhibits truth indeed. This is what we mean when we say that such a work is "true to life."

"True to life" is, unfortunately, an over-employed phrase which, because of a cultural sloppiness in our use of language, has gathered unto itself two meanings. The other, more common and less correct, seems to mean "reproducing everything just as it appears in real life." We have found how far away from the truth this can be. Besides, to reproduce *everything* just as it is in real life is to record life itself. Even if it were possible, is this the function of the artist?

Now we run head on into what appears to be an insoluble paradox. We pointed out that truth is really indivisible. A half-truth is not truth; truth out of context or out of time or personal relationship is not truth; truth embellished in any way is not truth. On the other hand, we know that art is achieved by selection, recreation, acceleration, stylization and a host of other deviations from observable actuality. If we accept the idea that that which is true conforms to reality, then how can we identify a work of art as conforming to reality or presenting reality if it does indeed diverge from all the facts? How can it be true?

The solution of this apparent paradox lies in recognizing that in posing the question in such a way we are really trying to make the beginning and the end of a process equal and identical. It is a basic human need to organize all of our experiences, on no matter what level they may occur, and to conceptualize our relationship to the reality of our experiences. This means that each new set of perceptions and responses, as they present themselves, are new bits to be added to the mosaic each of us is continually building in order that, internally, we can more and more completely represent to ourselves a world in which we can operate, a world which, by seeing it ever more completely and more meaningfully, we can with less and less uncertainty attempt to control, or with which we can, with less and less failure, be able to cope. Perhaps there are open spaces in our mosaic into which the new bits—those new perceptions and responses—can be put. Perhaps the bits already there can make more meaningful arrangements for us if they are moved around so that room is made for the new bits. If so, we have been able to modify our view of the world, enrich it, by accommodating to the new bits of reality. This is growth and the hoped-for purpose of education. The process of mosaic-building is continuous, commensurate with our lifetimes, and is limited only by death or some other proscription to growth that prevents us from including in our mosaic any new bits that might come along.

It is out of the continuous process of organizing all of our experiences, the process of mosaic or Gestalt building, that our experiences come to have functional meaning for us. The means by which we can "cope" in our world is continued reference to those meanings. We express those meanings as concepts and arrive at them through a kind of abstractive process that we call conceptualization. Once we have developed our conceptualizations of the real world, these conceptualizations, together with all manner of sensory and emotional memories, become our criteria, our measuring rods, by which we judge each confrontation in the world every day.

For the making of his artwork, the artwork-maker selects what are for him the most salient elements of his particular mosaic-like image/interpretation of reality. He works only with those elements he has selected. For him they are clearly representative of the reality of the world as he perceives it and responds to it. The selection and emphasis do not, for him, destroy the truth, the basic realities as he perceives and accepts them. The selection of elements, which may omit many details, perhaps, of his total mosaic, nevertheless represents the essential reality as it exists for him. The selection of elements represents the essential structure of his mosaic.

When the artwork confronts *us,* then we of the audience must respond to the selection of elements even though they may have been presented to us in stylized, perhaps re-arranged, composition. If we accept the artwork as conforming to *our* sense of reality, if we accept it as being true, it is because the elements that are there, in whatever manner they are presented, generate a resonance in corresponding elements in each of *our* mosaics. This resonance, serving to reinforce, intensify, to make more vivid, our perception of our own individual mosaics, confirms our sense of perceiving truth and at the same time gives us a sense of reassurance and exhilaration which is part of the art experience.

But what of the act of selecting and arranging the elements? How do we make the selection in the first place?

[1] *Film Technique and Film Acting*, V. I. Pudovkin, trans. Ivor Montagu, Vision Press Ltd., London, 1954, p. 140.
[2] A most instructive analysis of the technique, skill and effectiveness of Nazi propaganda films with special reference to the distortion of truth through the dynamics of cinematic construction is to be found in Kracauer, Siegfried: *From Caligari to Hitler*, Princeton University Press, 1947, pp. 297 ff.

CHAPTER III

The Necessity and Consequences of Making Choices

Every act that we perform is the result of our having made a choice. The choice may have been a totally conscious and aware act; it may have had very little or very great preconditioning; or the choice may not have been voluntary or conscious at all. The film-maker, like the maker of anything else, begins by choosing what he shall make; even, indeed, whether he shall make it! Then he becomes concerned with materials, form, style, use, audience or user, cost, and a host of other kinds of problems as well.

The means by which the maker of anything carries out his choices lie in his skill in the use of his tools and his materials. Such skill is his minimum equipment. Virtuosity, which is only a particularly fluent, practised mastery of such skills—a mastery which is always maintained by the skilled worker—is simply the basic requirement of any maker of things who is to achieve or retain first rank.

We are social beings. Our learning consists of the collected and condensed experience of society, as reported and interpreted to us, enlarged, enriched and interpreted by the collected and condensed experience each of us has enjoyed (or suffered) in contact with society. We cannot help learning the social meanings *for us* of efficiency, beauty, utility, economy, for, as members of society, we jointly and severally educate each other.

Thus our skills or virtuosity are learned within society, even though they may be used "against" it. But it is not the virtuosity itself which can hurt or build society. Virtuosity has only one function: it is the means by which someone has the capability of making or doing something well.

Society is the name we use to designate a group of living beings—usually human beings. Its size is of virtually no importance. A society can consist of a family, a clan, a tribe, a village, a cosmopolis or a nation. Each of these groupings is a kind of module in a larger grouping. Without reference to our choice in the matter, if we had any, each of us is a component part of the series of modules into which we are born or move. By being a constituent part of our immediate module, our birth into it changes it, no matter how minimally. Every change in even the smallest module changes everything of which it is a part.

There is no such thing as a one-way relationship. Every relationship is changed, modified, affected by all the parties to it, and, in turn, it changes, modifies, affects each of the parties involved. This is not limited to human relationships. The chisel used by the sculptor modifies the stone and is itself modified by the stone: it becomes dulled! The butt of the chisel is struck by the hammer and is modified by the hammer: it mushrooms, as does the hammer because of the chisel's resistance. The muscles of the sculptor expend energy in striking with the hammer and they become stronger by doing so. The mind and emotions of the sculptor direct the modification of the stone through the use of the muscles, the hammer, the chisel; and, in turn, the mind and the emotions of the sculptor are themselves moulded further by their creative involvement in the work itself. Just as the employment of his skill modifies each thing the maker makes, so the content of the thing that is made—that is to say, its use, beauty or aesthetic value, its relationship to its audience or its user, the material from which it is made and the manner in which it is made—condition the way the maker uses his skill, his tools, his materials.

As society changes by our growth and by what we make and do, as well as by the birth, growth, death and acts of every other constituent part, so society's modification, its effect upon us, changes us. From the skills and knowledge he learns in society, and from the attitudes he develops in society, the maker of things sees his relationship to society. The things he makes, whatever they may be, serve to "materialize" that relationship as he sees it. Through his awareness of the things he makes and his awareness of their relationship to society—and to the extent of his awarenesses—the maker of things further clarifies his definition of himself. To the extent that we are truly aware of our definition of self, of our relationship to our society, and to the extent that we conduct our behavior consciously as directed by our awareness, to that extent can we consciously change our society. To the extent that we consciously change our physical, geographic, economic, ecological and social environments, to that extent do we also change ourselves consciously, making us more capable of changing our environments still further.

All of the earliest documentary film-makers were middle class; in fact, almost all the early makers of all kinds of film were bourgeois. Joris Ivens was the son of the owner of photographic equipment stores in the Netherlands; Jean Lods was a musician in France; Alberto Cavalcanti, the son of bourgeois parents in Rio de Janeiro, became a graduate architect in Europe. John Grierson was the son of a schoolmaster in Scotland, and Robert Flaherty was an agent in Canada for Revillon Frères, the international furriers. Even in the Soviet Union, Sergei Eisenstein had graduated as an architect in Riga and Vsevolod Pudovkin was a chemical engineer. Is there some relationship between the ways such men as these were involved with the new film medium which they explored and expanded and the backgrounds from which they came? Each of us can come to his own conclusion, but let us suggest a few questions.

Is it not possible that the selective isolation of the prototypical characters in Cavalcanti's *Rien Que Les Heures,* as well as the clear reflections of a number of pervasive art movements of the early 1920's—Dadaism, Expressionism, for example—could only have been realised by someone who had been sensitive to and trained in the arts? Cavalcanti was an architect who lived in Paris and was very aware of his artistic environment.

Is it not probable that Ivens' film *Rain* was preconditioned by familiarity with and love of the work of the Dutch and Flemish painters? Is it not likely that the visual interest in the operation of machinery, which appears in Ivens' film *The Bridge,* was heightened and further stimulated by his studies in Dresden of the operation of cameras and of lenses at the Zeiss factories at Jena?

Is it not likely that the vivid sense of design which infuses all of Eisenstein's films was crystallized in his studies of architecture and his subsequent experience in scene design for the legitimate theatre?

Is it not to be expected that John Grierson, schoolmaster's son who studied social sciences and communications, should have spent his life attempting to educate the world with the newest communication medium of his time?

Unless we deny the possibility that any of these backgrounds exerted any influences on the film-makers, we must realise that the choices the film-makers made in the making of their films were, in some way, not totally free. They were not aleatory, they were not by chance. The choices that were made came out of the history of each of the individuals.

Just as the personal history of each of the artists helps to form that artist's criteria for making choices, so also do the availability of tools and materials and the other circumstances surrounding his engagement in producing an artwork. In the 1930's, the decade which saw the great growth of British and American documentary films, circumstances in Britain and the United States were very different. In the face of the Great Depression and the volume and salesmanship of the American film industry, some technique had to be found to protect the British film industry. A quota system was instituted which demanded that a certain number of minutes of each program in each cinema theatre in Britain had to be devoted to British-made films. The number of minutes so set aside was on a sliding scale increasing periodically over several years. Since the beginning of the scale was a unit far too short for a theatrical feature, room was made in the theatrical programs for the exhibition of documentaries (without that express intention, however), because the time slot was just the right length for this kind of film. In addition, Grierson persuaded the government to establish two production units, which, one after the other, financed and supported the production of documentary films. The British Empire Marketing Board set up a film unit to make films that would help to stimulate trade between the various Commonwealth countries; and when this was eventually wound up, Grierson, who had been its head, started the General Post Office Film Unit.

There were all of the circumstances for the fecund growth of documentary films: financed production units, exhibition possibilities, a most successful "operator" to steer the production units around the various governmental shoals. At the same time, because of this particular combination of circumstances, the pressure was to make interesting, moving, attractive films that might only *imply* their educational content, because they were exhibited in entertainment theatres.

In the United States, things were vastly different. There was no theatrical exhibition possibility unless it was in the very occasional art theatre. Non-theatrical, non-fiction films had been made for some considerable number of years for the U.S. Department of the Interior, for example, and for the U.S. Department of Agriculture, but these films were almost exclusively straightforward instructionals which seemed to owe more to the non-aesthetic tradition of classroom instructional films than to anything else. Additionally, these films were usually exhibited in specially assembled groups, or meetings, for which the arrangements had been made by the appropriate government department. During the decade of the 1930's, the decade of the Great Depression and of the Great Labor Union Organizing Movement, the Great Period of Social Questioning, there arose in the United States a new stimulant for the arts: the WPA Arts Projects. None of the arts could be free from the influence of the Arts Projects and the sense of "social consciousness" which pervaded them. The times, it appeared, were ripe for social duties to be undertaken publicly and a number of the great philanthropic foundations became quite active in financing documentary films. In terms of whatever definitions the foundations found valid or useful, these films were all of "social value." However, these documentaries were almost exclusively exhibited in "arranged" showings, as were the government films. Almost never were they exhibited theatrically.

The Arts Projects were not involved with feature films, nor, for that matter, with short films. Did Hollywood see to that? But Hollywood films did indeed accept some very considerable influence from the Arts Projects. An obvious example is *One Third of a Nation* which had been a legitimate theatre production of Halley Flanagan's Federal Theatre Project—one of the Living Newspaper productions. It was turned into a feature film starring Sylvia Sydney. Was it another Hollywood syndrome that, in this new form, the social message of *One Third of a Nation* was watered down? Those who are film buffs or who used to be addicted to late night movies are aware of how many films made at this period of time dealt non-romantically with the various aspects and conditions of the Depression.

Is it accidental that the films that were financed by the foundations and made by bourgeois intellectual film-makers were for the most part didactic? Is it accidental that films such as these relied for the most part on instructional narrative, albeit of high literary quality on occasion? Is it surprising that Pare Lorentz, the poet, made poetic documentary films?

Background and current environment appear to exert very considerable pressures, pressures that focus interest and attention in certain directions, pressures that seem to predetermine modes of responses. Are we then so boxed in that we really have no choices, *or no really voluntary* choices?

We may develop the following paradigm: The meaningfulness of every perception is in terms of the associations and relationships it arouses in us with other perceptions out of our pasts. In order to assure that no pre-imposed pattern of association govern our present perceptions, we must continue to question those present perceptions and the processes by means of which they come to have meaning for us. Since all our judgments are based upon criteria that are exercised by each of us individually, those judgments must be considered subjective. (It was to compensate this subjectivity and to replace it with consensus—perhaps closer to "objectivity"?—that the jury system was invented a couple of millenia ago.) Since our judgments are subjective, we owe it to ourselves and to our colleagues in society to be aware of the processes by which we have arrived at our criteria and the manner in which we apply them. It is only by continued questioning that we really become aware of them. Through this kind of awareness, we are enabled continually to test our perceptions and judgments in the light of new experiences and new judgments—which, through the dynamics of our own continued growth, will also continue to affect and change our perception process, our very perceptions and our criteria. In essence, we are thus continually refining our perception of reality. By testing every experience, every interpretation, every exercise of criteria—a testing performed by relating our experiences, interpretations, judgments, to a dynamic, growing perception of reality—we arrive at our own individual dynamic perception of truth.

It has only been through this kind of questioning and testing process that the great documentarians named in this chapter have achieved, each in his own way, individual perceptions of the reality of the world, innovative attitudes and judgments, and dynamic responsive behavior, very often in contradiction of the perceptions and values that their personal origins and backgrounds might well have dictated.

If we simply follow the dictates of our backgrounds and upbringings, allowing the choices to happen without question, then we are not really *individuals*. We become the building blocks for that autocratic, monolithic, conforming cultural-social entity that democracy abhors. On the other hand, we cannot deny that each of us has had a unique background and upbringing that, in combination with those of all our friends and neighbors, provides a wealth and a wisdom that should never be jettisoned. We must simply learn to understand what is involved in the shaping of all the criteria that we exercise in making all of our choices.

We must become and remain aware of our environment and our relationship to it, that is to say, our identity. We clarify and continue to refine the definition of ourselves by continuing to ask questions of our perceptions, of the meanings to us of each of our choices, our judgments. We must continue to ask questions about the effect each choice or judgment has upon the criteria upon which we made it. How are our criteria further modified by each choice, by each judgment? Questions are, in a very real sense, more valuable than answers. As film-makers, as film viewers, as people, it is certainly our obligation to ask questions continually of ourselves, for this kind of dialogue with ourselves is the way in which we grow.

CHAPTER IV

Product or Process?

In the tradition of half a millenium of scholasticism which prefers to treat all things as terminate and discreet, and in a society which is organized for the purpose of producing and selling commodities—each of which is also terminate in form and discreet—it is not surprising that we should continue to treat very nearly all of our ideas as if they, too, are discreet one from another and as if the *things* with which those ideas deal serve each its own single, unique function. This habit of thought may be further reinforced by our European-American culture of production, for, in this society, very few people are engaged in the actual making of artifacts. Our employment lists for job openings and jobs wanted, for example, describe lathe operators, sewing machine operators, punch press operators. No employer looks for someone who is expert in making spindles for chair legs or for banister or porch railings, no one seeks for craftsmen experienced in making sieves or ladies' blouses. There is a distance between the fabricator and the things he or she fabricates. The worker is almost always a provider of a *service,* rather than being a craftsman-producer. The output of one department of a factory provides the service necessary for another department to operate: the output of one factory or industry provides the service necessary for another factory or industry to operate. Even in microcosm, the exertion by one worker of his skill-competence on one unit in the production line provides the service necessary for the next worker in the line to exert his skill-competence. For a vast number of people in our society, the relationship between the maker of a thing and the thing that is made no longer really exists. The industrial worker is even paid without reference to the things that he makes. He is paid on the basis of time spent in doing his job, as though he were receiving a kind of recompense for penance, or he is paid for the number of units that pass his station on the production line, as though he, too, were a machine.

There are clearly tremendous implications in such basic alienation, implications that have immense psychological and philosophical import. Let us forgo further comment on these, at least for the present, and address our attention to the relationship that exists between the artifact and the artisan, between the artwork and the artwork-maker, because this is the relationship that also exists between the documentary film and the documentarian.

The process of making an artwork or an artifact appears to have two somewhat distinct parts, each of them requiring the artwork-maker to make and respond to a series of choices.

The first part of the process is that in which the initial choice of "what" must be made. That is to say, the artist decides first that he shall indeed make something and, further, he decides what it is that he will make. The choice may not be entirely that of the artwork-maker. The making of the artwork may have been imposed upon him in some way. He may, because he likes to eat, have accepted a commission to make this or that thing. He may, in order to win a competition or to fulfill some other kind of professional obligation, have accepted a specific task. But even these are also choices: he can accept or reject the commission; he can accept or reject the obligation.

Having arrived at this point, the artwork-maker finds that his choice of thing-to-make has already included a number of built-in parameters. He knows the subject of the work, that is to say, he knows its intended content. If it is some kind of dramatic work, such as a novel, play, film, or poem, he has some idea of what the major character may be, or perhaps the situation or locale of the action. If the presentation is involved with expressing certain ideas, these become the "what" the artwork-maker has chosen. If the artifact is to serve a purpose, perform a function, such as serving as a jug or as a button, this may be the "what." It may well be that the audience to whom the work is to be presented has also been described as an attendant parameter, as has the budget that is available and the amount of time the artwork-maker may devote to the preparation of the work.

No matter what the subject matter may be, no matter what the "what" may be that the artwork-maker has chosen, no matter what the parameters may be that have been described by his client, his supervisor or the artisan himself, once this set of choices has been made very little attention is paid to them as the work progresses. After that first set of choices has been made (or accepted), it serves only, perhaps, as part of the criteria by which the artisan judges and controls his work in process. For once he has agreed to the "what," all of the attention of the artwork-maker is focused on "how"—how shall he make the "what."

In the Clark Lectures of 1969, V. S. Pritchett, the British author and literary critic, says it this way, when talking of the creative work of the novelist: "The writer's work is a perpetual business of chipping off, a long process of rejection . . . Anyone who has written a story or novel is painfully aware of this. If *what* he has to say has been given to him by God, Nature, Society or Literature itself, the *how* of saying it will be his daily preoccupation."[1]

To some extent, of course, as we have suggested previously, the criteria on which the choices are made may have been provided by the inherited background of the artisan, or they may be impressed by the environments in which he has lived. Or the artisan may be innovative and creative enough to have questioned his heritage and his environment and have developed his own criteria. In any case, he now devotes his attention to solving all the problems of the "how" as those problems present themselves.

That which adds the art-ness to an implement, tool, instrument or other artifact is indicated by the general term "aesthetic." Those qualities which, lying in the "how" the artwork is made, generate sensuous and affective responses in us are said to be aesthetic. In each medium the means of achieving aesthetic results are different because they must clearly depend upon the tools, materials and mode of viewing, hearing or use. In each medium there are elements which can be selected, arranged, manipulated, to provide some kind of aesthetic stimulus. These elements are simply the aesthetic elements of the medium. In order to illustrate, one can point, for example, to some of those aesthetic elements which occur in painting—color, line, mass, texture, and further arrangements of such elements by repetition, variation, sequence, leading to rhythm, harmony and so on. In music, although texture has a different meaning, there is texture, melody, harmony, pitch, timbre, and more. The selection and arrangements of the aesthetic elements and of the elements of the subject matter generate structure, aesthetic structure. Not all of the possible elements available to him may be utilized by the artisan. A musician may not use all of the orchestra: he may use a sexet, or a quartet, or a duo or only one instrument. He may use a relatively complicated melodic idea, like the series of a twelve-tone composition, or he may use the almost irreducible "dit-dit-dit-dah" on which Beethoven built his Fifth Symphony. (It is unnecessary to emphasize that the extraordinary qualities of Beethoven's Fifth Symphony do not arise from that "dit-dit-dit-dah," which is the "what" of his composition, but rather from what he has done with it, *how* he has treated it. It is the "how" that counts.)

In making a film, of course, the film-maker has a host of aesthetic elements from which to draw, even in a documentary film where he may not have control of locale, setting, costumes, cast or even plot.

From the time he has accepted the "what" until the work is completed, the artisan, the artwork-maker, the documentary film-maker, is totally devoted to the "how" of his work. For him the choices that he must make, one after the other, compose the whole of the process of *making* the work. Each choice is in actual fact his answer to a question, his solution to a problem, and each problem deals with how to make the aesthetic "package" more clear, more intense, more effective, more successful. It is the solving of these problems that is the act of creativity and it is the process of solution that engages the artwork-maker's interest and attention.

The problems to be solved are not apparent all at once. One or several of the problems, for which his solutions become manifest in his choices, may appear at the beginning, but each solution, each choice, generates subsequent problems, subsequent solutions, subsequent choices. At such time as the end of the series of problems appears to be at hand, that is to say, at such time as the artwork-maker sees no more problems between himself and the task of completing the "how," he begins to lose interest in the work itself. So many painters and sculptors, shortly before the completion of a piece of work, find that its completion is really a kind of unpleasant chore. There are no more questions, no more problems, so, because there is no more search for solutions, there is no more creative activity. At this time, the artwork-maker has found that his interest is now focused on the task of selecting the next "what."

This is not really to say that the artisan has no other interest in the finished work than the solution of its aesthetic problems. That would be both simplistic and untrue. But it is true that his interest in the finished work, indeed his interest in finishing the work, is very largely extra-artistic. He has been rewarded by perceiving, in the eyes of his mind and his feelings, the solution of all the problems he has set himself in accomplishing the "how" of the artwork, even before it may have been actually completed. But he may seek other rewards, such as kudos, dollars, fame, reputation (valuable for ego support and for subsequent commissions) and is pleased to finish the work for any or all of these reasons: he may also be impelled to finish the work because of some kind of moral drive or habit of work that has led him to abhor an unfinished task. The reasons for finishing it are not really "intra-artistic" reasons, that is to say, they are not related to the aesthetic problems and solutions that have constituted the creative process of making the work.

Thus it seems fair to say that the artwork is, for the artwork-maker, a point in time, a kind of frozen moment in his process of aesthetic problem-solving.

On the other hand, this is not meant to imply that there is no involvement of the artwork-maker in the "what-ness" of his work. He may, as Picasso did in his painting *Guernica,* have worked towards the generation of the shrieks of pain he himself felt in the destruction of this quiet Spanish village by the Nazi bombing planes; or, as Jean Rouch, have attended to interpreting some aspect of life in an African town. There is a continuing reflexive interaction between the "what" and the "how."

Let us refer back to Grierson's definition: "The creative treatment of actuality." What is meant by creative?

When children play they remember, from day to day, their successive play experiences and often repeat or vary their play on following days according to the success—or satisfaction—

of earlier days' play. The play itself has, as John Huizinga describes,[2] a number of qualities: it is voluntary, it gives fun and is indeed undertaken because of the fun it generates in the players, it creates a new, make-believe reality that is encapsulated within the rules of the game and the acceptance of the players and this make-believe reality is apart from "real" reality. To Huizinga's characteristics I would add that since children are social beings it is not surprising that their play is in large part mimetic, and that it begins and proceeds, building its rules and its progress, by means of free association. One idea or action generates another that leads the play on. Clearly, association can only occur in terms of past experience which, for humans, is by definition social experience. The player is a social being whose associative process depends upon social experience (interpreted by the private, personal response of the individual!).

Creativity has many of the same characteristics as play. It is voluntary. It gives pleasure. It develops its own reality, differentiated from "real" reality (for this is where the basis of innovation occurs). It proceeds by means of the solving of problems suggested by free association: but, whereas in play the free association is not checked or "censored," in the creative process the selection of problem and solution is based on the need to integrate each problem and its solution with the needs of the "what" and the "how" of the work and the needs of other problems and solutions in the completion of the work.

As with the child, so the artwork-maker. The associations can only be in terms of past experience which can only have occurred in terms of his total life in society. No one can divorce himself from the effect of society upon himself, as we have said earlier, any more than he can prevent himself from having effect upon society. Thus the criteria by which choices—that is to say, solutions to problems—are made can only be generated in relationship to society.

The meaningfulness of any perception for the perceiver can only be in terms of what he brings to the encounter. Everything that happens to me can only have meaning to me in terms of the meaning to me of everything else that has happened to me. Since I cannot avoid living in some kind of society, everything that I encounter, everything that happens to me, everything that I happen to, is a social phenomenon. Thus meaningful perception determines meaningful choice-making for the individual who makes the choices and this meaningfulness can only come out of the social environment of the choicemaker.

When the spectator-auditor—whom we will call "respondent" from now on—encounters an artifact or an artwork, the process we have been describing is inverted. If enough interest has been generated to demand from the respondent even the briefest attention, he will become aware of two kinds of things which engage him. He deciphers and relates to the "what-ness" of the work, and he relates to what he *feels* as a result of the total encounter. If the work is an artifact for us, this presents the respondent with a variety of judgments, choices, to make. He will make value judgments concerning the effectiveness, the efficiency, the use-value of the artifact; and he will, partly as a result of his relationship to these judgments, and partly as a result of the aesthetic qualities he finds in the artifact, make further relational perceptions and further value judgments. ,

If the work is an artwork, the same kinds of involvements engage the respondent. He relates to the "what" of the work, which is to say, he discerns the meaningfulness of the "what" to him; and he responds to the feelingfulness, the aesthetic qualities, of the work. On the basis of criteria that he has acquired up to the time of the encounter, the respondent makes value judgments about the work.

As the work is a kind of demonstration for the artwork-maker of his solutions to a series of problems, so it then becomes a kind of generator for a series of problems to be solved by the respondent. Because no two people bring the same collection of experiences and responses to any encounter, no two people can have the same perceptions of the encounter. The maker's perception of needs, purposes, the "what" of the work and his perceptions of the problems to be solved and the choices, or judgments, that lead to his solutions, cannot in any way be identical to the respondent's perceptions of the "what" and his perceptions of problems, requiring solutions, choices, judgments.

In some areas there will be some similarities in the criteria used for making these judgments. Some of the criteria are based on conventions accepted by the society which the maker and the respondent may share. Such community may be in cultural tradition and convention, sub-cultural convention, or historical contemporaneity. In many broad aspects choices made by artwork-maker and by respondent may appear very much alike. However, since each is an individual who responds to his environment in his own way, each will develop a coloring or overlay to his criteria, or his application of them, that does indeed differentiate the judgments and choices made by the artwork-maker and by each respondent. Thus, no matter how we might wish it to be otherwise, it is not possible for any communication, even if we extend this to include artworks and artifacts as well as all other kinds of symbolic expression or statement, to be a simple transitive process. Communication cannot be like the transmission of a pile of dirt from one place to another by a steam shovel. On second thought, perhaps it can! The arrangement of the dirt, the relationship between its parts and particles, cannot remain unchanged! It is basically a philosophic truism to say that movement and change are identities, whether or not the movement is of things concrete like rocks or things abstract like ideas.

[1] *George Meredith and English Comedy,* V. S. Pritchett, Random House, New York, 1969.

[2] *Homo Ludens,* a study of the play element in culture. John Huizinga. Beacon Press, Boston, 1970, pp. 8-9.

CHAPTER V

Objectivity vs. Aesthetics

Objectivity, as the word is usually used when talking of documentary films, seems to mean that the material of the film, its subject matter, is presented just as it occurred, without any distortion. It can be assumed that distortion is not a matter of degree. Any distortion removes objectivity. Purity alloyed is impurity. If this is not so, then objectivity has no meaning.

The progenitor of all modern documentaries, *Nanook,* was made in 1920. At that time it was accepted as a film that did indeed present the Eskimo, Nanook, objectively and was praised without limit for doing so. Unfortunately, it was replete with physical distortions! First, it was black-and-white; yet, unless we are color-blind, we see the world in color. Second, it was silent; yet, unless we are deaf, we hear the world. Third, it is a two-dimensional representation of a three-dimensional world. Fourth, it would only be by sheerest accident that our seats, when viewing the film, would place us so that Nanook would really be life-size (as seen from our distance from him). Fifth, the translation of the world of color into the world of black-and-white was made on a film stock called orthochromatic; that is to say, *Nanook* was a motion pictured photographed on a photographic emulsion that was color-blind to red, an emulsion that did not translate red into shades of grey, but only into black. Sixth, the running time of the film was not commensurate with the represented time of the action; that is to say, the real time of the film as it passed through the projector did not equal the real time of the action. A new time period, which we now call *virtual* time, was created. Seventh, a new geography was created, much as virtual time was created, by arranging the shots of the film. Eighth, unless the focal length of the projector lens was twice the focal length of the photographing lens and unless, under those circumstances, we sat exactly halfway between the projector and the screen as we viewed the film, we could not see the same perspective as the photographing lens. Yet, no one is disturbed by these deviations from "actuality," to use Grierson's word. What, then, is actuality if it is presented with so many mechanical and physical distortions? (In passing, it may be noted that in the review of *Moana*, from which we have quoted earlier in this book, Grierson notes the great improvement made possible by the use of the new *panchromatic* film, a film bearing a photographic emulsion that *was* sensitive to red and therefore translated reds into shades of grey.)

These distortions, these deviations from "objective" presentation, are accepted by all of us as viewers. Because we have accommodated ourselves to them (in the sense that our eyes "accommodate") we disregard them; they become quite unnoticed.

However, the major part of the problem is whether or not film-maker or film viewer are aware of the distortions. The distortions themselves are always with us. There is never an absence of optical distortion; there is never an absence of temporal distortion. Indeed, there is never an absence of color distortion, for even in color film there are only three colors from which all the colors of the photographed scene are "mixed."

Every one of these deviations from "actuality" is, in fact, an abstraction. A two-dimensional representation in color of a three-dimensional object is an abstraction, perhaps not quite as abstracted as a black-and-white two-dimensional image. An even greater degree of abstraction is the stick figure that is frequently used in cartoons. But, regardless of the degree, all are abstractions.

Abstracting is the process of "drawing from" the whole some of its parts. We abstract the wheat from the chaff. In a pictorial representation, clearly, the purpose of abstraction is to strip away those elements which are considered to be less important in order to emphasize those elements which are considered to be more important. Time, space, color, and similar kinds of elements, when emphasized or arranged, can greatly intensify our feelings during the viewing of a presentation. This is what is meant by aesthetics, for the word "aesthetic" simply means "feeling." (Note that the opposite of *feeling*, "NOT *feeling*," is expressed by the word "anaesthetic." The Greek word "aesthetic" is made into its opposite by the Greek prefix "an-" which means "not." Thus, aesthetic is the opposite of anaesthetic.) Aesthetics deals with the aspects of the presentation that generate feelings in us, the respondents.

When the World Union of Documentary Film-makers phrased their definition to say, as we quoted earlier, that documentary film should "appeal either to reason or emotion" they did not consider that in "real life" reason and emotion, cognition and affection, are not alternatives, one to the other. No one ever learned anything without a feeling for doing so! If the learning took place because of some external pressure—the need to pass an examination, the need to satisfy someone else, the need to get a better job or get an increase in pay, or just the need to satisfy the social pressures of one's community—the meaningfulness to self of the material learned is diminished, perhaps absent altogether. In those circumstances, the feelings associated with particular learning experience, or with that particular art work confrontation, are quite extrinsic to the work itself.

When, however, the confrontation occurs between learner and things-to-be-learned, or artwork and respondent, and the feelings are generated by qualities within the work itself, we can say that the feelings are generated intrinsically. There are qualities within the work, intrinstic to it, that generate feelings in the respondent. These intrinsic qualities appear to fall into three different categories. The respondent may be excited by the subject matter of the work. He may empathize with it, or sympathize with it, or find it anathema, but for whatever reason, he is moved by the subject matter, the material, of the work. The respondent may also be deeply (or not so deeply) moved by the attitude of the artwork-maker to the material as that attitude appears to be exposed to the respondent by the presentation. Lastly, the feelings of the respondent are stimulated by the aesthetic packaging of the presentation. In motion pictures, this means the creative functional use of the kinds of distortions that we spoke of earlier, as well as many other ways of dressing the work. This may include the way in which each frame and sequence is composed, the manner in which pace and rhythm have been given to the presentation; in fact, all those qualities which make up "how" presentation has been made, about which we have talked in a previous chapter.

None of these three basic sources of stimulation for our feelings—subject matter, attitude of artwork-maker, aesthetic package—works by itself in generating feelingful response in us as respondents. Perhaps it is because of a strong response to the subject matter that we continue to attend to the work that we are further moved by what appears to be revealed of the artwork-maker's attitude and is reinforced by the aesthetic elements employed. Perhaps it is some one (or group) of optical or auditory attention-getters that catches our attention, makes us pause to consider further the material of the work and, through this, gain some kind of perception of the artwork-maker. No matter what it is that first draws us to continued attention of the work, we become further enmeshed by our perceptions of the elements in the three major areas we have described; and our cognitive, thinking, reasoning activity becomes intensified by our feelingful involvement, while, reflexively, our feelings are intensified by the "information," the cognitive burden, of the work.

In "real life," we do not separate our feelings from our thinking. This is simply a trick of language. We have not yet learned to speak, nor to understand speech, contrapuntally. Each of us is endowed with only one soundbox and we can speak only one note at a time, one word at a time. Therefore it happens that when we are describing something that has more than one attribute simultaneously we are forced to speak of those attributes sequentially. The sequence is demanded by the nature of our language and of our learned ways of understanding spoken and written language. Cognition and affection, occurring simultaneously, nevertheless are spoken of in sequence and linked with a conjunction. We then, because of the habit of language use, begin to think of the two actions—cognition and affection—as happening separately and sequentially.

This coexistent interrelationship can be demonstrated negatively as well. Clearly, if our attention is not drawn and focussed on the work by reason of our having been caught up by at least one of the aspects in it—subject matter, sensory attraction (sight or sound), and so on—we do not continue our attention, we do not respond to the work. We are "turned off." We have no stimulation of our feelings; we gain no "information"; we have no interest in the work.

Recognizing, then, that any presentation distorts actuality in ways that can be used to generate more intensive feelingful response, we can arrive at only one conclusion. We relinquish our identities as individuals if we allow the existence of such distortions to remain unused, undirected, non-productive. We cannot, by the nature of film, for example, avoid making a film that contains a variety of distortions, as we have already discussed. The nature of the technology predestines this. We are left with either not noticing their presence and pretending that there are no distortions, and that, therefore, it is possible to make an "objective" presentation; or with being humans who are aware of our environment and the occurrences that take place within it, and because of this awareness recognizing that the medium of motion pictures does indeed present "actuality" distorted.

The first alternative turns us into ostriches: we do not see any danger if we keep our heads in the sand and refuse to become aware of what is about us. The great discomfort of emulating ostriches is, of course, that we present a certain portion of our anatomy to be belabored by real "actuality."

The second alternative, our recognition of the deviations from actuality that the medium itself presents, directs us to make use of every quality, characteristic, attribute, element, that occurs in the medium. Regardless of what we may think about the desirability of "objectivity," the presence of which we have demonstrated cannot really exist, we have for hundreds of years nevertheless accepted a general agreement or consensus that the more the artwork-maker is aware of all the possibilities open to him in manipulating the aesthetic elements, and the greater the degree to which he manipulates them in order to make an artwork that is most effective in generating an affective response, feelingfulness, in us as respondents, to that degree is the artwork-maker a superior craftsman.

Thus we find that we do indeed look for the craftsman to distort the "actuality" of this material, and when this distortion is "well" achieved, we are pleased and say that the craftsman is a good craftsman. So we have thrown objectivity out the window, or at least we have denied the need of objectivity as far as actuality aesthetically distorted is concerned.

CHAPTER VI

Objectivity vs. Citizenship

Modern civilization in western Europe and North America—the only civilization about which I have the competence to speak—appears to generate the most stringently polarized controversies while abhorring the publication of anything "controversial." The prohibition of the broadcasting of controversial programs, both on radio and on television, is almost universal in our western civilization, although there is some variance from one country to another of the line of demarcation between what is permissible and what is not.

Presumably the fear of broadcasting anything controversial is the fear of disturbing or annoying some part of the audience, or, in commercial broadcasting, of disturbing or annoying some paying advertiser. It has become a cultural habit to fear "making waves."

In film classes the existence of attitudes and points of view is the focus of much discussion. This is true not only in the United States but also in France, it seems. In the early spring of 1973 in Paris, Jean Rouch invited me to attend classes he was conducting in the subject "Ethnology and Film." M. Rouch is a Professor in the University of Paris, and his classes were held on Saturday mornings in the theatre of the Cinémathèque Française in the Palais de Chaillot. I took advantage of the invitation to attend three successive classes. The discussions that took place among the students of this class of Jean Rouch seemed to be replications of discussions which students in my own classes engage in, year after year. M. Rouch's students, as well as my own, appear to be deeply exercised by the problems of what is reportage, what is documentary; what is real and what is actual; what is truth in film; what is education and what is propaganda. Because these problems are not yet solved for the students, there is deep concern over how much of the film-maker himself is to be expressed in a documentary and how much "objectivity" is to be sought.

One of the manifestations of some of the partisans is the large degree of reverence accorded to data. There seems to have arisen a cult of data-fetishists, for whom their data are more desirable than any use to which it might be put. It is evident in the need that is expressed for works that are totally "objective reporting" or "objective recording." There is something comforting, it seems, if bias is neither overt nor even discernible. The appearance of not presenting a bias can also be given when the maker of the work includes every possible attitude that he has come across. He, the maker of the work, leaves it up to his audience to "make up their own minds." He has shown himself in this way to be "objective and without bias."

It is also somewhat astonishing to discover that bias, which is the cause of this kind of prohibited controversy, can occur only in the moral, the political or the economic arenas. This is not very surprising since it is relatively clear that politics, which deals with economic and legal, as well as social, relationships, and morals, which generally provide a metaphysical rationale for the present western European world order, are really aspects, therefore, of the same thing. On the other hand, conflicting theories about the origin of the universe generate a controversy among such a small portion of the total population and deal with virtually no part of the present order of society in our infinitesimal portion of the universe that they appear without let or hindrance in print and on radio and television. In the same way, superficial controversies are openly sought in the name of freedom of speech so long as they do not deal with anything really fundamental. For example, it is permitted to exhibit or broadcast various views about prison reform so long as the continuance of prisons and their underlying philosophy are not threatened; one can say almost whatever one wants, to as large a public as one can generate, about whether or not there should be a large or a small armed force in one's own (or somebody else's) country, so long as the idea of international hostility as a viable method of solving international economic or political problems is not really basically threatened.

The compulsion to refrain from publication in print or on the air of anything "controversial" is justified on the grounds that presentation without bias permits the audience, as we have said, to "make up its own mind." The value of the "objective" reporter, the unbiased reporter, is elevated for the same reason. Some doubt has already been cast on the possibility of being unbiased or objective, but, if it *were* possible, we find that the result would be three alternative paradoxes. The first is that it is politically desirable not to be political, not to express a political attitude. The second, even stranger, is that it is morally preferable not to express a moral preference; it is morally proper not to take a moral position. And the third is the observation that the only person who can really separate himself from involvement in the world is the psychotic—or God! Surely, all others who have to earn a living, in order to eat and be housed, who must have some ideas about their fellowman or they would find it impossible to publish anything no matter whether in print or on the air, cannot resist developing attitudes about all the things in which they are engaged. After all, hopes and ambitions are value-based expectations; the person who is without hope or ambition is considered to be severely traumatized.

Granted, then, that everyone who is a member of society and who is not so traumatized that participation is denied by reason of serious disability, what must the direction of each person be? The humanistic attitude is stated by Pablo Casals. In a broadcast honoring his eighty-eighth birthday he said: "Only to live is not enough; we have to take part in what is good. We must react—to accept, to refuse. The privileged must take part in the movement of the world, the ideas of the world. Participation in the world is good—it is necessary."[1] And again, on the same occasion: "We must think of ourselves as the leaves of a tree, and the tree is all humanity. We cannot live alone, a leaf without the others, without the tree, without the earth."[2] The recognition of participation is stated by German Nobel Laureate in Literature, Heinrich Böll, when he says: "All publishing, even a poem, is a political act because it's public."[3] For Böll, there is no choice in the matter.

We have already explored the necessity of participation in an earlier chapter. The choice *not* to participate is just as much a choice as the choice of *how* to participate. It is inescapable that not to choose is also a choice! The choice not to participate, it seems to me, is the search for the "comfort" of not having to exhibit a commitment; but it is a choice made without the recognition that the resultant lack of participation is indeed the exhibition of an attitude.

It would seem to be evidence of the wish to become invisible, or, at least, indistinguishable. No one notices any individual grain of sand because, from a small distance, each grain looks like any other. If I don't make waves and don't draw attention to myself by being different from my neighbors in any way, perhaps I, like a grain of sand, can remain indistinguishable.

Unfortunately, indistinguishable in this kind of context leaves us bound within a terrifying syllogism. If we are all alike, we cannot be identified one from another; thus, we have no individual identity, and—haven't we all been painfully seeking for it? Members of armed services are dressed all alike so that they will have no individual identity, so that they will be depersonalized. The process of depersonalization was brought to its most intense resolution under fascism, for it is in fact the purpose and the result of a fascistic outlook. On the other hand, depersonalization is also total alienation, both social and psychological. The depersonalized member of society is the automation of Fritz Lang's *Metropolis,* the mechanicalized workers. Depersonalization results in lack of sensitivity to, indeed lack of recognition of, one's neighbor. This is alienation, but it is also a psychosis!

Thus, the wish to become indistinguishable is the wish to become a depersonalized, alienated element within a kind of fascistic structure; or, it is the wish to become an alienated psychotic; or, it is both.

One of the ways our society reinforces the idea that objectivity, lack of bias, is desirable is by the emphasis it puts upon the acquisition of data. The acquisition of data has become, in fact, tantamount to "education." A very large proportion of our educational examination process deals with the ability of the student to regurgitate data. The objective examination (note the term!) is based upon closed, fixed, unambiguous answers that are only arrived at by the regurgitative process, for the objective examination—whether true-or-false or multiple-choice—can be graded by a moron; for all that is required is a template which is laid over the examination paper with holes through which are exposed the *only permissible right answers,* or the examination papers are punched through each right answer (found by template) and the punches are scored by a punch-card machine. One might say that this kind of process provides an examination "untouched by human hands"—and, most certainly, one that is untouched by human minds. But it does have one great advantage. There is no room for a single variant opinion; nor for a single "right answer" to be doubted. In this way, we arrive at objectivity, scientific impartiality, the only valid educational goals—that, at least, is the rationale!

This leads us to clarify just what it is that we mean by "education." If we mean that each student must be trained to provide the same response to every question—for that is precisely the goal towards which almost all of our elementary and secondary schooling leads—we are obviously directing our efforts to developing a society made up of those who can push the buttons and levers and pedals of Lang's *Metropolis;* but by no means endangering them or us by teaching them to think! If, however, education means helping young people to prepare themselves to make a better world than the world we put in their hands they can't very well do it on the basis of our answers which have so clearly demonstrated that we have failed in a great many ways. If our answers were not outstandingly successful, their continued application won't improve them or the world toward which they are directed. If education is aimed at making people into robots like those in *Metropolis,* we shall have people who make things and never even see the things they make, let alone use them. But, we have already pointed out that separation of maker from thing-made removes the maker from the chance of developing his identity; for the sense of making, the sense of personally-having-made-it, is what basically helps us to differentiate ourselves for ourselves. Our society with its depersonalized production lines is already showing deepening stress-marks caused by alienating the worker from product-making and therefore alienating him from himself.

In our society, the compensation for this alienation takes the form of fantasy. Built into our social organization is the need to sell the things that society makes. This is done by a host of social pressures in addition to advertising in all media. But the makers of things, many of them, cannot afford to buy the things they make. Moreover, our society has become a society in which more and more of its members provide services instead of making things, and the servants cannot afford many of the things our society makes. This is not to mention the large number of unemployed who, obviously, cannot afford to enjoy the products of society. The pressure of salesmanship, however, affects all of society and those who cannot afford the good things that are being sold are forced to live in a world of dreams and wishes, a world of fantasies. This dream world is a world that is bounded by the knowledge that the enjoyment of the things dreamed of will never occur in reality within the structure society maintains, so that the dreamers are made passive and further alienated, or they find "anti-social" means of achieving what otherwise would not be available. Perhaps they rob or defraud.

On the other hand, if the output of our educational system were young people who had been helped to prepare themselves to improve the world in which they have found themselves, they might discover a better kind of organization than the one that has shaped them so far! The implications of an educational system, and of the society in which that system has been generated, in which such value and dependence are granted to the collection and display of data are extraordinary and somewhat frightening. Data, in our society, means all those "facts" that have been collected and stored, and, in relationship to students, all those facts that have been established by others and memorized by the students for instant replay. It seems not to have occurred to anyone that *facts, data, are the past.* They deal with things, events, relationships that *have* occurred. We live in a society, the new, atomic-age society, the new moon-landing-age society, and all of our educational focus seems to be on the past. There is a paradox!

If data are indeed the past, what, then, is the future? What good are data, for presumably all are not bad? Data, hard information, result as the answers to questions, and form the basis upon which inquiry is erected. Questions, inquiry—here is the future. Inquiry is not yet satisfied. It must be made clear that there are two kinds of questions of which one kind is in fact retrospective. The kind of question which only demands the "objective" regurgitation of data as its answer is retrospective; and it cannot really be called inquiry. It is very similar to the Pavlovian stimulus and is used to make certain that the conditioned response will be exhibited. Questions which do manifest themselves as part of inquiry, however, are future-directed and because of this have importance.

We have discussed the necessity of making choices and we have seen that choices are solutions to problems. We live our lives by making choices. Sometimes the choices are very large and include many smaller choices. The choice to remain indistinguishable, for example, is the answer to a lot of problems dealing with one's relationship to society and one's relationship to those who appear to have control over one's own part of society. Fears, anxieties, doubts, form the context within which this kind of problem is solved and the general solution is made that manifests itself in the choice of resisting or refusing commitment in order to achieve what appears to be a greater security through remaining anonymous. Nevertheless, if we are to be aware, productive humans, surely we must be aware not only of the phenomena that confront us all the time, but of the relationships among the things we see and feel and observe, and of their relationships to ourselves. Productive inquiry arises out of this kind of awareness and out of our questioning all of these relationships. Questioning the data isn't very important in itself, but questioning the relationship is. Sometimes this is triggered by the discovery of new data, but the new information itself has no great importance other than to make us aware of questions that must arise about relationships as we have perceived them up to the time of the new discovery.

Through the process of inquiry we can learn to focus our choice-making. If we seek to make our choices themselves relate one to another, then learning the process of inquiry helps us to focus our problem identification, our problem-solving, our choice-making. It seems clear that education based upon the collection and emission of data is turned backwards facing the past, and will produce people who do things the way their teachers do things and the way their parents do things. While in no way intending to derogate either parents or teachers, it is clear that somehow parents and teachers have failed to make a very desirable world for their children or students. For another generation to do things the way we have done things will serve no one well. If we, as parents and teachers, are beginning to question our ways, how much more important, even imperative, it is to help students to learn how to ask questions, to learn the process of inquiry, and direct them, not to the past, but to the future.

The answers we have used in our generation of parents and teachers, even if they were at that time more right than has been demonstrated, will not work in the world of our children and our students because that world continues to change. There are more people, using more things, in less space, with less clean air and less clean water, and with less food being produced and a rapidly increasing shortage of protein, for example. The problems that our children will have to address themselves to solving are different from the problems that we perceived. Our answers and our ways, doubtful in the past, cannot be appropriate to the new problems, and it is only through inquiry that we can help the generation of children and students to recognize and become able to cope with their new problems.

Those citizens, those documentary film-makers, who have felt strongly the need to address themselves to making a better world are those who have affirmed that documentary film is an art of advocacy. The only question that was asked of me by John Grierson when I presented myself to him as a candidate for a job with the National Film Board of Canada is demonstrative of this. Grierson asked me: "What do you want to *do* with film?" He was not interested in whether I knew at that time, in June of 1941, anything about films in general or documentary films in particular. He was not interested to discover that at that time I did not know that there was photographic emulsion to be found on one side of the celluloid. For John Grierson documentary film was a tool for education, for propaganda.

Paul Rotha states the position unequivocally. "Daily jobs, no matter how well described by rhetoric of camera and intimacy of microphone, are not documentary material in themselves. They must be related to the wider purposes of the community."[4] And again: "The essence of the documentary method lies in the dramatization of actual material. The very act of dramatizing causes a film statement to be false to actuality. We must remember that most documentary is only truthful in that it represents an attitude of mind. The aim of propaganda is persuasion and persuasion implies a particular attitude of mind towards this, that or the other subject . . . your documentary director dare not be neutral, or else he becomes merely descriptive or factual."[5]

These quotations bring us face to face with another generator of fear in our western European and American civilization: the word "propaganda." The word has acquired for itself a vigorous normative meaning. Anything that is labeled propaganda is dangerous, false, frightening. Somehow the word has become one of the strongest pejoratives in the language. Yet, missionary services for various churchly sects are called propaganda missions; salesmen call the supportive material provided them in all kinds of media "propaganda." In neither of these highly restricted uses is the pejorative quality conveyed. The original Latin word simply meant "those things which are to be propagated, which are to be spread about, enlarged." There was no normative intent whatsoever. My mother recognized the new accretion to the meaning and said: "When you teach me what I want to know, that's education; when you teach me what I don't want to know, that's propaganda." Even allowing for the fact that some pejorative quality is intended to be conveyed by the word, why should we be afraid of propaganda? We only need to be afraid of propaganda if we have not yet learned to ask questions, for, as soon as we are willing to question what we are being told, we have the chance of finding the fallacies. Again, the need for questions and inquiry is emphasized.

The scientific method, to which we are repeatedly directed to make obeisance because it is objective, is so because it is, in Rotha's words, "merely descriptive or factual." It may, on occasion, go beyond this and become analytical, although analysis can also lead into the pitfall of making value judgments and thus lose it objectivity. But the very need to continue scientific exploration is based on value judgments, both social and personal. There are social climates that generate attitudes of approbation of the researcher. There are ambitions and hopes in the feelings of the investigator. These are not objective. They are highly subjective drives, occasioned by personal reaction to the researcher's environment or his society. It is impossible, as we have said earlier, for us to relate to our environment without developing preferences, likes, dislikes, fears, securities, all of the paraphernalia that go into the making of value judgments. Without all this, we are really the mechanical men of *Metropolis,* the alienated, the psychotic. For us to deny part of ourselves in the making of judgments, in the making of our work, is to deny that we exist as participating humans in a human society.

The work of making films, for instance, consists continually of making choices, of exhibiting preferences. How is it possible to make the choice of this shot or that, this camera angle or that, this kind of cutting or that, without relating the choice-making to our own sense of relationship to society and environment? To attempt to seek the "freedom" of wished-for objectivity is really to seek the strictest kind of confinement, the narrowest kinds of parameters. By really being aware of the world, by really knowing *for ourselves* what is real, we simultaneously reject images given us by others and images we develop in our own fantasies. Our recognition of reality as it exists *for us* is a very real maturity. It is a maturity that gives us the greatest range of freedom within which to make our choices and our films.

A continued awareness of reality gives us the flexibility to cope with the changes in our environment and in ourselves that our own choices make. As we have said, aware choice-making ensures that we can change our personal environment as knowing, aware citizens; even our resistance to making choices is a choice that modifies our environment in some way.

We have the alternative of making these aware choices, of seeking to modify our environment knowingly, or of resisting voluntary choice-making. We have already discussed the problems attendant upon this resistance. However, an aware, participative member of society must have what are for him productive social attitudes and value systems and he must, by the nature of his own participation, be willing to commit himself to the choices he directs himself to make. It is for this reason that we denied that advocacy is within the definition of documentary, but advocacy might well be a criterion by which we value a documentary film as being a good documentary or a bad one. If we value a member of society who continually relates to what he perceives in society, as it is and as it changes, and if that member of society exhibits his awareness through the choices he makes, then it follows that we value the work through which his choices are made evident. Those who are not participative are, as we have shown, pawns or psychotic. It is not possible for a participative citizen, by definition, to refrain from making choices, from exhibiting choices, from having preferences and basing his actions on them.

As that is the case, it is not possible for the participative citizen to make a film of any kind—and this includes a documentary film—which does not exhibit his point of view about his material. Even the simple choice of putting the camera *here* to make the shot instead of *there* is an explicit choice of point of view.

Objectivity and participative citizenship are not compatible. It is clearly a denial of the obligation of citizenship of a film-maker, as it is of any citizen, to demand that he exhibit no commitments, that the film-maker or artist be caponized or spayed and, by being half-selves, do only half their work. To paraphrase what might well have been said by Gertrude Stein, a complete citizen is a complete citizen is a complete citizen; and a complete film-maker is a complete citizen is a complete film-maker!

1 *Casals at 88*. One hour special program, Columbia Broadcasting System, December 14, 1964.
2 *Ibid*.
3 *Germany Restored*. An interview with Heinrich Böll by Alice Fleming. *Intellectual Digest*, May, 1973.
4 *Op. cit.*, Paul Rotha, p. 133.
5 *Op. cit.*, Paul Rotha, pp. 133-134.

CHAPTER VII

Film and Anthropology, or, What is Style?

The subject matter of documentary films is, we have agreed, the various relationships of mankind in this world—the relationship of man to his environment, man to his work, man to other men, these relationships taken singly, or in any combination. From this we have further agreed that a simple collective term for this kind of subject matter is anthropology. The motion picture camera, however, cannot take pictures of relationships as abstract ideas. Motion picture film only records pictures of things and people as they live and work in relation to each other. This is where the final, total and irrecoverable loss of objectivity occurs. We must learn to recognize that this is not a hindrance nor a deprivation. It is the only way in which we can make our films artworks.

Everyone places the camera in such a way as to take a picture of the material that will exhibit most clearly what is happening. But—who decides on the meaningfulness of what is happening and what aspect of what is happening needs to be exhibited? The individual members of the audience have not spent time in the company of the participants of the action to be filmed, so all of the ambience and all of the preparative and predisposing conversations have been denied them. The film-maker knows this. He must make a film that will explain, demonstrate, illustrate, illuminate, what is to be happening through his filming of it.

Does he know what kind of meaning the subject will have for each member of his audience? Not very likely. He can, at best, know its meaningfulness to himself and on the basis of this he must make his choices.

This necessary kind of subjective criterion leads to strange ideas. The question was put in a somewhat different context during one of Jean Rouch's classes: "Is a film made by an indigenous film-maker likely to be the same as, or different from, a film made by an outsider, a stranger?" The meaningfulness for the viewer who is a member of a society will not be the same as the meaningfulness for an outsider, no matter how benign that outsider may be. An analogy can be seen in the drawings of people by little children. When a three-year-old, or a four-year-old, draws pictures of his parents or his aunts or uncles, his figures are not only stick-figures, but their proportions are quite strange. All the legs are very long, all the torsos are very short, but all the heads are quite large. This is so universal that one becomes very certain that the reason for the distortion is not because of some lack of ability to coordinate the hand that holds the pencil with the eye that sees. The reason is much simpler. The distortion arises out of the child's point of view. When he is standing facing his parents, the child sees legs. His head is perhaps only as high as his parents' thighs. No more. From the standing position, the child's view is only legs, and, with head turned upwards in order to see the faces of the grown-ups, their torsos appear foreshortened, far less long than is "really" so. The even further foreshortening of the head is compensated for by the child's knowledge of the face gained from so frequently sitting on the grown-ups' laps. For the child this kind of proportion that is evident to him is very real. It represents the real world that he knows. For him it is objective reality and the objectivity is "proven" by the universality of this distortion as it appears in children's drawings. If objectivity is attained by consensus, then this is objective reality for all children. Yet, it is not objective reality for their parents. In the same way, a film-maker indigenous to the group being filmed will see the group differently from the way a film-maker who is not a member of the group. The reality of the group may appear very similar to *all* indigenous members but very different from the appearance of reality to the outsiders. There is a kind of group subjectivity which arises simply out of the cultural meaningfulness of the encounter.

This kind of group view, cultural viewpoint, is one of the most important aspects of the study of anthropology, for it is out of this cultural view of the world about them that each group builds its own ways of dealing with the world. The ways in which a group deals with the real world, real as it appears to the group, is called the group's "life style." Almost the whole content of anthropology concerns itself with studying life styles, the life style of work practices and work habits, the life style of family relationships and sub-group relationships, the life style of religion, of art, of war.

Group style, then, in perhaps somewhat oversimplified terms, is the behavior pattern developed by the group in dealing with the world as they see the world. Thus, life styles, or group styles, occur as cultural responses to the world. As anthropologists, we are interested in learing how different groups address themselves to the task of making the world work for them. This is the task of anthropology, and it is undertaken so that we can know more about the world ourselves.

Two things emerge from this. It is "we"—whoever that may be—who study "them." No matter how we might wish it otherwise, this contains an elitist center from which the studies and the attitudes about the studies, even the attitudes that originate the studies, grow. It was because of this essentially elitist origin that the need to question one's attitudes continually and in depth has been emphasized. It has only been because they, too, questioned themselves and their relationships to society, that some of the great documentarians who have been named in earlier pages became great documentarians!

The second thing is the fact that whatever we find out about the world modifies our attitudes about the world. Sometimes it takes a long time and a lot of information to make basic changes in our attitudes to the world, but, over the years it does happen. From the Ptolemaic world view, additional knowledge about the world brought Copernican attitudes; and from Copernicus our world view was changed by the new knowledge about the world in the time of Newton; and today the attitudes initiated by Einstein and developed by others have opened up the universe, only to bring sufficient changes that new attitudes still will be bound to develop.

The attitudes that a culture holds are evident through the ways they are externalized in behavior. We learn about the attitudes of the group through the ways in which they do their work, through the ways in which they collect their food and house themselves, through their rituals and their arts. We begin to understand the meaningfulness of the behavior to the group by relating its parts together. Then, since we cannot understand without finding the meaningfulness to ourselves, we relate what we observe to what we do, to how we behave. This process of learning to understand what we observe by relating it to what we do is also reflexive. By relating what *we* do to what we observe, we learn to understand more about our own behavior and our own attitudes. This further understanding of ourselves changes us. If the understandings and the changes occur through our conscious attempt to be aware, the skills that we learn in order to achieve them are called "perception skills." Perception skills are those through which we learn to recognize and identify, to find meaningfulness in, more and more of what confronts us, more in quantity and more in detail.

The differentiation between cultural groups seems to arise because of some kind of isolation which the group has found. The limits may have been set by the supplies of food that have been available, by the need for protection from the elements or from other predators, or by any of a host of other reasons. It is the isolation that provides the environment for somewhat unique problems to be solved and special ways of perceiving those problems and solving them—problems dealing with how to make the world work better for the majority of the members of the group. As the group becomes larger and as parts of it therefore differentiate themselves from other parts, subcultural patterns grow up. This is because the needs of each of the subgroups become sufficiently different that the problems of making the world work better for them are perceived somewhat differently from subgroup to subgroup. The attitudes begin to differ, the questions begin to differ, and the solutions, made evident through the behavior of the subgroup, begin to become discernibly different. Susanne Langer, on the opening page of *Philosophy in a New Key,* says:"Every age in the history of philosophy has its own preoccupation. Its problems are peculiar to it. . . . The 'technique,' or treatment, of a problem begins with its first expression as a question."[1] These problems, these questions, arise from the ways in which the relationships in the world about us are perceived.

The technique of solving a problem, of dealing with it, is expressed in the ways in which questions about that problem are put. The form of a question, which represents the form of a perception, is in fact a styled expression. Style is the manifestation, through the quality of behavior, of the perceptions of problems and the techniques of solving them. We have seen that cultures and subcultures develop styles. We have seen that historical epochs have developed styles. It is clear, also, that individuals develop styles. The highly creative person seems to have the capability of escaping more from the bonds of his cultural and temporal prison. He is less bound by the ways of perceiving problems and solving them that have been developed by his culture than his fellows. He sees the world differently and therefore the problems that he must face appear different. He finds new techniques in order to solve the problems in new ways. Indeed, it is for this reason that we have come to regard innovation as one of the characteristics of creativity.

Each of us, whether film-maker, member of subject group, member of audience, is, for better or for worse, a human being. Each of us has grown up in a group, perhaps in a subgroup. Each of us has been exposed to the pressures of perceiving the world in certain cultural ways. Each of us has been exposed to culture pressures to perceive the problems within the world in a common way and to solve those problems in a common way. Thus, each of us reflects the style of his culture and subculture. To the degree that each of us has learned to resist the pressures of our cultures and subcultures, each of us may have developed creativity, the ability to perceive differently from the group, to express questions differently from the group, to solve problems differently from the group. Each of us then has developed some kind of individual style.

But, since we are either film-maker, film subject, or audience member, we approach the tasks imposed by *that* particular relationship and solve the problems of those tasks in our own personal and individual styles. Each film and what we see in it occurs for each of us in terms of our own styles. Thus it is that style, personal and cultural style, cannot be avoided in the making of a film nor in the viewing of a film, nor in the responding to a film, or to any other confrontation, for that matter. For these additional reasons, then, it is not possible for us to respond to the world, nor to make films, without bias. We cannot be without attitudes. If objectivity means to be without bias, to be without attitudes, it is an impossibility. If objectivity means to give all sides of a question and thus present the *appearance* of not having bias, the impossibility is no less apparent. Each of us who has the desire to present all sides must first make *his own* identification of all those sides, and, for his film or other work, must identify the sides that he will use. He must choose to select or to collect, and he must make the choice of what should be included in the collection and what should be left out. All these choices are based on criteria that are determined by the group or the subgroup, whether or not those choices are modified by the resistance of such a person to those cultural pressures.

Objectivity isn't possible on aesthetic grounds. It isn't possible on anthropological grounds. It isn't possible if one is an active participant in society, who is relatively free from psychosis! What is possible?

The only productive alternative is the recognition of the realities. It is only here, in the recognition of these realities, that freedom lies, freedom to avoid the pressures that one's society imposes. If we do indeed recognize the cultural and historical pressures that weigh upon us and direct us, then we can question them. By questioning those pressures, we give ourselves the opportunity of perceiving the world in new ways, of perceiving new kinds of problems and developing new techniques for responding to the problems, new techniques that are, in Susanne Langer's words, expressed in their own kinds of questions. Our answers to those questions, as seen in our resultant behavior, can be described in terms of style, new styles for new times.

What of style in anthropology? What of style in documentary? It follows all that we have said above. Our view of our material and the questions we ask about it determine our style. The more creative the anthropologist, or the more creative the film-maker, the more personal must his style be. We learn to recognize the work of this or that creative personality by the marks of the personal style that are evident in the work. We have come to expect this in the films we call "creative." (as opposed to those we call documentary!). Luis Buñuel is identified by a highly personal style that we have come to classify as "surrealist." He makes his images express the fantasies of the characters in his stories, images that often emerge as irrational free-associations, dreamlike. He has made films of this kind for nearly half a century. He has, however, made a documentary film, a totally anthropological film, that deals with a small village, Los Hurdos. It deals with people living isolated in the mountains of Spain west of Madrid. The film is expositional and interpretive of the people of Los Hurdos, people who are profoundly poor, profoundly undernourished, illiterate, inbred, quite without hope. The people suffer so deeply and are so marked by their suffering that they seem to be the population of a nightmare. Buñuel remained within his style notwithstanding that, in *Land Without Bread,* he approached an anthropological subject as any anthropologist might be expected to have done. It is his material that appears surrealistic.

But this is not the only example of identifiable style, nor the only way in which style can occur, in documentary films. In Rouch's class, already referred to, comment was made about Buñuel's counterpoint of ethnographic reporting, interpreting, against surrealist images. A question then arose: "Is there the possibility of counterpoint between the symbolic language of film and the symbolic language of the material, the people of the film? Or, on the contrary, must we have a symbolic language in film?"

It is impossible to make a film without selecting at least some of the elements—places to put the camera, things to include in the shot or to exclude from it, the way to cut from one scene to the next and how long to leave each scene when the cutting is actually done. There are, as we pointed out earlier, other cinematic exigencies that make it impossible to reproduce actuality—whatever that might be. Selection and distortion are unavoidable in making a film. Selection and distortion create abstractions, however. We select those aspects of our material that will most readily, or most forcefully, demonstrate whatever our film is to demonstrate. Since we cannot avoid distortion, we use it for the same purpose, to demonstrate readily or forcefully whatever we are to demonstrate. By leaving out certain aspects of our subject material, if only because of the exigencies of selection, by emphasizing some aspects and minimizing others, we are abstracting from the whole actuality those parts of it that "suit our purpose." We have in this way developed a symbolic language. We express the life styles of our subject material, in documentary films, through this symbolic language. Any life style that is identifiable by relatively fixed behavior patterns or its rituals has also developed its symbolic language. We express this set of symbolic meanings through the use of another symbolic language.

Just as our understanding of a culture other than our own helps us to understand our own, just as defining the world around us defines us in the process, so the use of one symbolic language to express the meaning of another culture, another set of symbols, illuminates both what is to be expressed and the meaning of the symbols in the language used.

The arts are particularly viable media through which to explore, express and respond to documentary subject matter: people and their relationship to the world. Data, as we have said, represent things past. It is very difficult to be involved in what is past unless that past has happened to us. We have little or no emotional identification with it. Reading books or reports that provide us with data engage us in an almost totally cognitive occupation. The arts have the common characteristic of their feelingful presentation in addition to whatever content they may bring us. The feelingfulness, the aesthetic, of the work involves our emotions, our feelings, as well as our intellect. The sense of involvement we find within us is of "now." The sense of involvement with data is "time past." Future is always imaginary, intangible. (The intangibility is emphasized by the fact that our language has one word to indicate present time: "now"; and one word to indicate *both* time past and time yet to come: "then"!) The future is born in our questions, in our inquiry. The "nowness" of the art experience also has a sense of "here," and it is these two senses, "now" and "here," that involve us so deeply and intensify for us the meaningfulness of the experience, and the meaningfulness of the content of the experience.

[1] *Philosophy in a New Key,* Susanne K. Langer. Harvard University Press, Cambridge, Mass., 1967, p. 3.

CHAPTER VIII

What Happened in a Course on Documentary

Introduction

From September of 1967 until September of 1972 I served as organizer and Chairman of the Motion Picture Department of Columbia College in Chicago. During that period, the general area of motion picture history was dealt with in terms of generic focus, rather than chronological period, ethnic center or the works of one director or another. In the fall of 1971, Motion Picture History dealt with Documentary Films. Since I had begun my career in film more than thirty years before as a documentarian at the National Film Board of Canada under the late John Grierson, and since a department chairman can arrogate to himself the privilege of teaching his own preferred courses, I elected to teach Motion Picture History: Documentary.

At each meeting of the class, films were shown and discussed. It is my way of teaching to do so inductively and discussion is the core of this mode of teaching. While it appeared appropriate to present the subject of documentary in a generally chronologic frame, in order to draw attention to the development of ideas and attitudes, it was equally important to make sure that the films offered to the students for study came from a wide variety of societies and that a variety of styles and modes of film statement be exhibited. We were particularly fortunate in that, through the kind services of the French Film Office, it was possible to invite one of the great artists of world documentary, Alberto Cavalcanti, to appear at the College, to have him present some of his films, and for him to discuss them with the students. He came to us the last week of the semester.

Among the films presented on the occasion of Cavalcanti's visit were *Rien Que Les Heures*, a reenacted, dramatized documentary about Paris made in 1926; *Squadron 992*, produced by Cavalcanti and directed by Harry Watt for the British Ministry of Information in 1940; and Cavalcanti's most recent film, a *Life of Theodore Herzl*, made for the Israeli government and for which the photography was completed one week before the Six-Day War in 1967. The students saw almost half a century of film-making by one artist, films about a wide range of people, places and social problems and attitudes.

A few months earlier, in June of 1971, Jean Lods, another great documentarian from France, had visited the College with some of his films. A number of our students in the class had taken advantage of his visit to see the films and to meet and talk with him. Still earlier, in January of 1971, the students had the outstanding privilege of meeting with John Grierson who had also come to talk with them and to take part in discussions with them. The semester at Columbia College was 16 weeks long. We therefore had to provide for 16 programs. Our time period was from 6:30 to 10:00 in the evening, a period ample for the viewing of a feature-length film and a generous discussion. The films were drawn from standard repositories: e.g., Contemporary Films/McGraw-Hill; Crowell-Collier, Macmillan; Film Images; Museum of Modern Art; and others. Descriptions of the films, including all pertinent material, are to be found in the catalogues of the repositories.

As a general rule, it was our wish to provide programs with some generic integrity on each evening and, in the list which follows, the focus of such grouping is indicated.

WEEK	TITLE

1   *Moscow Clad in Snow*
    Man With a Camera

    The first week showed simple record photography contrasted
    with Dziga Vertov's and his Kino-Eye.

2   *Rain*
    Granton Trawler
    Nanook

    Very early, very simple social observations recorded with the
    eyes of lyric poets.

3   *Berlin, Symphony of a Great City*
    Gamla Sta'n

    The socially involved films of the city presented with a high
    sense of visual design.

4   *New Earth*
    The River
    Grass

    These three films deal with the elements of the earth and the
    way in which we relate to them.

5   *Moana*
    Le Tempestaire
    Le Mistral

    Stylized approaches to viewing natural elements and
    subjective relationships.

6   *Bambini in Cittá*
    Thursday's Children
    A Child Went Forth
    Children Adrift
    My Own Yard to Play In

    A wide variety of statements about children.

7   *In the Street*
    Housing Problems
    Enough To Eat
    Land Without Bread

    Films dealing with food and lodging.

8 Visiting Lecturer

On this day we were fortunate to have a visit from Zelimir Matko, the managing director of Zagreb Films in Zagreb, Yugoslavia. This film studio specializes in short subjects of two quite disparate varieties, namely, animation films and socially involved documentaries.

In a previous visit, Mr. Matko had provided our students with a program of animation films, and so it was a most happy opportunity to have him present and discuss documentary films made by his studios in our course in documentary film. This was especially valuable since Mr. Matko acknowledged the debt owed to John Grierson by documentary film-makers in Yugoslavia. John Grierson had visited them on more than one occasion.

9 *Dead Birds*

Anthropology in a Stone Age culture. This film deals with a ritualized state of war which exists permanently between two tribes in New Guinea.

10 *Beaver Country*
Louisiana Story

A modern lyrical view of nature and the impact of industrial society.

11 *Turksib*

A documentary about the building of a railroad from Turkestan to Siberia.

12 *Report From China*

A recent feature-length documentary about the China of today.

13 Visiting Lecturer

Relatively few film-making students attempt to use film as a means of interpreting the world about them and their relationship to it. Dr. Ernest Rose of the Temple University Motion Picture Department founded his department with a declared emphasis on the making of documentary films. On this occasion, Dr. Rose visited Columbia College with a program of documentary films made by his students.

14 *Le Retour*
    Night and Fog
    Films dealing with the aftermath of World War II.

15 *Battle of Algiers*
    A documentary in which all of the facts are historically verifi-
    able but in which all of the scenes are totally reenacted.

16 Visiting Lecturer
    A visit from Alberto Cavalcanti, which has been described
    earlier.

About halfway through the fall semester, 1971, I announced
to the class that there would be a term paper to write. I proposed to the members present that they should suggest, and we
would discuss, then and there, appropriate topics on which the
paper might be written.

As I have said, it is my custom to teach inductively, so the
idea of proposing that the class generate a set of appropriate
topics was not traumatic for them. It wasn't even particularly
surprising. We have frequently discussed, in our classes, the
fundamental need of all of us to learn how to conceptualize.
My students now know that this is, indeed, one of the most
basic skills one should learn in college (especially since it is a
skill that is generally not learned earlier). Their suggestions for
term-paper topics came out of this background.

As one might suspect, there was not a unanimous accord
with the idea of writing a term paper in the first place, and one
student complained that it really wasn't right to ask for a term
paper in such a course. I replied that I would be pleased to
accept, as one of the topics, a discussion of the validity of a
term paper in a study of documentary film. Someone else asked
how long a paper should be and I gave my stock reply: "As long
as you have something important or interesting to say." It
turned out later that only two students finally discussed the
validity of a term paper in this course, and neither of them had
made the original verbalized complaint.

During our discussions of the filming techniques employed
by Robert Flaherty while making *Nanook* and other films, and
the equipment and techniques used during World War II at
the National Film Board of Canada, the students knew that

equipment had changed over the years, as had modes of film-making. It was suggested that perhaps there might be an exploration of what difference might be generated in the relationship between the film-maker and his subject when the interface between him and it—the way in which his equipment might allow him to approach it—varied.

For purposes of our conversations in class, and based on my own documentary experience, I had given my students my definition of documentary: a film which deals with the relationship between people and environment, people and work, people and people (or any combination of those relationships) as seen in any society existing at the time the film-maker makes his film. Nevertheless, some of the students had either not really understood the implications of this definition or had not been completely happy with it. It was suggested that a term paper might develop and defend a definition of documentary film.

Some of the more politically aware students wanted to discuss the function that documentary films might serve in terms of public education or in stimulating emotional or attitudinal change. Others, some of whom were socially aware and some of whom might have been timid of social or political purposes, wanted to explore the ways in which a film-maker ought to be responsible to himself and his audience.

Some of the students were practicing teachers of film courses in high schools, for Columbia College offers studies for film teachers to help them learn better how to teach film themselves. It was most appropriate that one of the topics dealt with developing an outline for a course in documentary film.

As each topic was proposed and discussed, it was distilled so that it could most clearly reflect the process of conceptualizing its content, and, when the suggestion and discussion of topics was completed, we had finally come to a listing of nine different headings. Each of them appeared to be capable of generating interesting and useful exploration. More important, they all had one other characteristic in common: no paper could be written simply by copying paragraphs or regurgitating information that might be found in books or easily available in journals. Each subject was what newspaper people call "a think piece." To be sure, reading source material never hurt anybody. In this case, it would certainly not be harmful and could very well provide demonstrative evidence for whatever thesis the student might offer. At worst, quotation would provide (in the words of Pooh-Bah, in Gilbert and Sullivan's *The Mikado*) "merely corroborative detail intended to lend artistic verisimilitude to an otherwise bald and uninteresting narrative." Primarily and necessarily, each paper could only be written as the result of serious and committed thought on the part of the student.

The final list of term paper topics was typed and given to each student. Here is a reproduction of it:

Term Paper Subjects
History of Film/Documentary
Fall Semester, 1971

The following subjects were generated by students in class as those subjects from which each student is to select a topic for his term paper:

1 Discuss the validity of a term paper dealing with documentary films.

2 Discuss the effect on the film and on the subject of the film caused by varying modes of interface between observer (filmmaker) and the event.

3 Discuss the relationship between documentary films, realist films, adventure films, romantic films, western films, detective films, etc., and truth.

4 Develop and defend a valid definition of documentary films.

5 Discuss the function of documentary films in the development of human awareness.

6 Develop goals, rationale, and a course outline for a course in documentary films.

7 Discuss the function of purpose in determining the artist's selection of his mode of expression.

8 Discuss the responsibility of the film-maker to his audience, to his subject, to himself.

9 Discuss the function of topicality in documentary films.

When all the papers had been written and submitted, something else was revealed. Some topics attracted far more interest among the students than others, and one, topic Number Seven in the list above, although suggested and discussed by several students before inclusion in the final list, was, in the last analysis, abandoned by all the students.

Each of the 57 students who submitted papers had demonstrated a determined application of his or her capabilities in dealing with the subject chosen. A number of the papers, by reason of original thought, clarity of expression and commitment of attitude, warranted public exhibition. It is those papers which compose this section of the book.

I hope it may have become clear that my own ideas have changed since I began to teach that course in 1971. One of the advantages of teaching is that one is forced to organize one's own knowledge and develop one's own concepts in order to articulate ideas for students and in order to have a base from which discussion can arise. One learns what one knows. However, the students themselves bring bright minds and develop good ideas, and these also work to change the ideas of the instructor. That is all for the better. My next course will be the better for having taught this one. Yet, it was teaching this one that made this book possible.

Because the course could be taken without prerequisite, the class was composed of a very wide variety of students who brought a very wide variety of experience to our discussions. There were people from a considerable number of different ethnic and national backgrounds, distributed among students who ranged from college freshmen to veteran, practicing high school teachers. For these reasons, the papers presented here do not compose an integrated, monolithic structure of ideas or attitudes. Indeed, some appear to contradict others, and, most fortunate, some appear to contradict me.

In order to make it possible to appreciate the context within which each paper was written—and thus make it possible to comprehend more completely the implications of each term paper—each author was asked to submit his or her own biographical résumé. No parameters were set for the form of these résumés and they appear with their authors' names as they were received.

CONSEQUENCE OF THE COURSE

Defining the Documentary Film

---

by Carol Eastman

A.B., Vassar College, **1961.**
Production Associate at Coronet Instructional Films, 1964-1970.
Teacher of American History, Francis W. Parker School, Chicago,
Illinois, 1961-1963.

Writers on documentary film agree on one attribute of that
form of motion picture: it is truly a document—recorded evidence or information. Frequently documentaries are called
"nonfiction films." John Grierson defined them as "the creative
interpretation of actuality" (p. 454).*

This actuality is a real event or a real place or a real person
or group of people, whereas fictional dramatic films are invented. There is a type of reality which fiction can express, and
that is the reality of relationships. In fact, the best fiction is
"true" in the sense that we recognize the pattern of relationships within it. Satyajit Ray states that this type of reality is
the proper province of the documentary (p. 381). It is the
invention of characters and/or places and/or times which
makes fiction different.

The camera does record what is in front of it. What we see on
the screen (leaving out consideration of optical effects) is pre-
sumed to be what the cameraman saw through the viewfinder.
So that if the camera is present during an event, the film deals
with the "actuality" of the event. Parker Tyler says that the
recording nature of the camera is the "one essential fact . . . at
the base of the documentary conception." (p. 253)

But this does not preclude the "actuality" of a real event being recreated for the camera. Almost all pre-*cinéma vérité* writers agree on that; the Academy of Motion Picture Arts and Sciences includes in its definition of documentary film the phrase ". . . either photographed in actual occurrence or reenacted." (p. 276) The difference between this re-enactment and fiction lies in the fact that fiction is invented. In documentaries, re-enactments are portrayals of real people, places and events.

Does this mean that historical re-enactments can be documentary? Parker Tyler discusses at length Eisenstein's *Potemkin,* which is a later enactment of an actual happening, as a documentary. But Satyajit Ray says much of the detail was invented and there was some change of setting; it is not "a faithful account of a historical event." (p. 381) What Eisenstein had probably done was to impose invention on an actual happening; *Potemkin* turns out not to really be a document because its veracity is challenged.

But another type of historical film can be called documentary: the National Film Board's *City of Gold* is an example of this type. Still photographs (or, conceivably, other graphic materials) contemporary to the period are the material used in making the film. (p. 303) The thousands of photographs of the 1896 Gold Rush in Dawson are a document of a real event; filming them does not lessen their actuality; it may heighten their drama. The endless single line of prospectors going through the Chilicoot Pass is a compelling shot in the film, much more so than the photograph.

The documentary film must be more than real, however; more than "an arid compilation of data" (p. 112); a newsreel may be a document, but it is not a documentary film. A central idea must be present; there must be all the ingredients of an integrated film of any kind: drama, conflict, an overall idea. Willard Van Dyke defines the documentary as "a film in which the elements of dramatic conflict represent social or political forces rather than individual ones" (p. 346). This definition is close to that found in the *American College Dictionary* (Random House, 1956): ". . . a film, usually non fiction, in which the elements of dramatic conflict are provided by ideas, political or economic forces, etc."

A good example might be Pare Lorentz' *The River,* which has as its protagonist the Mississippi River Valley. Individual people are not in the film. We see the effects of human presence on the river, and the benefits of the river on the people. The conflict comes between what the population has done to destroy the valley and what the river, both beautiful and generous, might be doing for the population. But the film's point of view is always with the river itself.

This is not to exclude the type of film in which an individual person is featured. *Nanook,* for instance: not only is one character and his family featured exclusively in this story of Eskimo life, but also a large part of the film is re-enacted. *Nanook* is generally considered to be the grandfather of documentary films, but later work has consistently moved away from its format.

Grierson says, according to Parker Tyler, that the ideal of documentary is "to draw men together into a homogeneous global group by portraying them so that the essential humanity of each nation will shine through its strange clothes and exotic habits" (p. 252). *Nanook of the North,* however re-enacted, however romantically portrayed, documents the struggle of an Eskimo and his family against the hostile Arctic environment. Non-Eskimos for the past 50 years have watched this struggle with interest and involvement. The very personification of the Eskimo in Nanook is what gives the film its universality. We know Nanook well; he is like us.

If a documentary film is one in which the elements of dramatic conflict are provided by political or social ideas, must the film show a social commitment on the part of the film-maker? Well, the existence of the film in the first place shows at least an interest in this political or social idea, and probably a point of view. No statement, be it film, word, or picture, can avoid a reflection of attitude; this is not exclusive to the documentary. The question is really whether the documentary film, by definition, must try to persuade or to generate action from the audience.

During turbulent times, socially concerned men speak louder than in placid times. The Depression of the 1930's brought forth all the frustrations of men who wished to see more radical social change. Many of them felt that this social change would not come about unless the filmmakers documented the conditions of labor. "The raw meat of social reality is a preferable diet to the creampuffs of Hollywood. This we know," wrote Robert Gessner in 1935 (p. 95).

World War II generated a great many films, paid for by the government, designed to produce enthusiasm for defeating

Hitler and produce behavior that would assist in the conduct of the war. The need for democratic propaganda in film was expressed by many documentary filmmakers. "I keep on feeling," wrote H. Forsyth Hardy, "that the documentary group as a whole is not at the center where political and social planning is being thought out and legislated, or not close enough to the center. It is not good enough to be on the outside looking in, waiting on someone else's pleasure for an opportunity to serve social progress" (p. 210).

It is obvious that many documentaries do generate action in the audience, and, depending on the circumstances, many of them are made with that intention. But some documentary filmmakers may only want to show an aspect of the world, as it is, for the understanding of those who are not aware of this aspect. *Song of Ceylon*, a beautiful film in its structure and composition, can be thought of as such a film. It is a document of the East so complete and complex that it must be absorbed in an Eastern way. Therein lies its brilliance, for to watch the film with total attention is almost to imagine oneself a part of Ceylon. The film is quiet and subtle. A documentary may aim only to show, not to convince, and do it with moving artistry. Julien Bryan tells of his filming of a particularly violent stage of the war in Warsaw: "What effect (these pictures) have, I do not know. It is not for me to draw conclusions. My job is to make pictures and this I have done. I have brought back, from a world gone mad, a record of war and what it does to people." (p. 174).

Many statements have been made about documentary films that are descriptive of the genre, but are not definitive. Grierson's "creative interpretation of reality" is one; it would be nice if all films were creative, particularly documentaries, but many are not, and they are still documentaries, though dull. The statement that a documentary is a film about people's relationships to other people, to their jobs, or to their environment is true, but not limiting enough to be definitive. It seems to me that a documentary film is one in which the elements of conflict represent ideas, either social, political, or economic, and in which the vehicle used to express these ideas is largely factual, rather than invented.

*All page numbers are from Lewis Jacobs, ed., *The Documentary Tradition from Nanook to Woodstock* (New York: Hopkinson and Blake, 1971).

The Differentiation of Modes of Interface Between Observer and Event

by Richard C. Haverstock

BACKGROUND: Born in Waukegan, Illinois. Moved to Chicago in 1950 and have lived in the area since then. Married; wife is an elementary school teacher. Two years of service in the U.S. Army as a military policeman, training NCO, and staff announcer and board man for AFKN (Armed Forces Korean Network) Radio in Pusan, Korea.

EDUCATION: Graduated Morgan Park High School in 1964. Attended Western Illinois University and Southeast Junior College, and, after flunking out of both schools, I was drafted. After my discharge I attended Bogan Junior College. In 1971 I was graduated with an Associate of Arts degree with honors. This is my first year at Columbia College.

HOBBIES: Tinkering with electronic equipment, still photography and darkroom work, antiques, and stained glass crafting.

To simply restate the title, one could call this discourse a discussion of the confrontations that exist between the filmmaker and his subject. These confrontations can run the gamut from total hostility to fear, mistrust, apprehension, anxiety, and hesitation. The subject has good reason to fear the filmmaker: his race, language, physical appearance, level in the social strata, and profusion of camera paraphernalia can all contribute to the alienation between subject, camera, and filmmaker.

The filmmaker can overcome almost all these fears that the subject might have. While he cannot readily change his physical appearance, he can overcome the language barrier with the use of an interpreter. A discussion of viewpoints between the subject and filmmaker can minimize both class and racial differences, but the documentary artist will always be hampered by his equipment.

The cameraman is a slave to the light: while his eye is able to adapt to a contrast ratio of perhaps 100:1, his film is capable of a 35:1 ratio at best. He is also a slave to his mechanical camera, full of intricate parts that freeze, stick, need constant attention and lubrication, and like neither temperature nor humidity extremes. His attendant sound and lighting equipment are equally as finicky, and need masses of connecting cables and electrical power to function. The concept that follows is natural: highly flexible and technically refined equipment, in the hands of a technically proficient and artistic filmmaker, can allow that filmmaker to produce better films. The ability to concentrate on the event and the filmmaker's reaction to that event is greatly aided by equipment that never intrudes on the event.

In *Making Movies—Student Films to Features,* Hila Colman differentiates between cinéma vérité (direct cinema) and the documentary film:

The documentary is the result of a process of selection. The filmmaker chooses images and sound from real life and sometimes restages real experiences against their actual backgrounds. He then shifts and organizes his material and with the help of a narrator explains it to the viewer. Direct cinema, however, is based on recording life as it exists at a particular moment before the camera, with the filmmaker never intruding by directing the action. He simply records what he sees and hears.[1]

Hila Colman also thinks that modern, more flexible equipment is narrowing the gap between direct film and the documentary.

Cinéma vérité is an outgrowth of the Flaherty tradition of making faithful film studies of the culture and customs of real people. After Flaherty's Nanook of the North, *filmmakers all over the world began to take their cameras on location . . . However, until there was a revolution in the equipment used, they were hampered by cumbersome camera and sound equipment. It has only been since new equipment was developed that the documentary filmmakers have been able to turn more to the concept of the direct film.[2]*

Richard Leacock (formerly one of Flaherty's camera operators) and his partner, Donn Alan Pennebaker, are considered to be leaders in this "direct film" type of documentary. After World War II service, Leacock went to work as a cameraman for Flaherty. He recalled, "The cumbersome and complicated sound equipment was frustrating. Too many wires and cables, too many people—inevitably it destroyed all you wanted to do."[3] But Leacock had majored in physics at college and had ideas of his own about developing more flexible equipment.

When Mr. Leacock went to Israel in 1958, he wanted to record what happened, "but the equipment was heavy, clumsy, and the quality was no good. It took half an hour to connect up the cables, and we were always too late to catch what we wanted." He vowed that he would have different equipment and began to develop a quiet, easily portable, hand-held camera which could synchronize with a small, quality tape recorder with no connecting wires. Leacock says, "Now two of us can do everything, one taking pictures and one sound. We carry everything wherever we want—no cables, no wires; it's run by batteries. We can film anywhere."[4]

Leacock returned to Israel in 1968, with Leonard Bernstein, to film a symphony performance. Concerning his new equipment, he said this:

It was the easiest thing in the world to film anything. We had three cameras that moved all over the place. No connecting cables, and we got beautiful sound. It was this new equipment that created the possibility of going out and observing. It makes any filmmaking easier if you take advantage of it."[5]

The idea of sound and the documentary film placed other limitations on the movements and settings of documentary subjects. Richard Shickel writes of the problems of sound in the early days of Hollywood.

Some of the effects of the sound revolution are well known: how actors whose voices did not "mike" well found their careers ruined; how the camera, so painfully taught to move, suddenly became static again, placed in a booth to prevent the microphones from picking up its whirrings; how the sound men for a while replaced directors as the guiding spirits of the individual movie to the vast—if temporary—detriment of the film art.[6]

The immediate effects on film form and content were obvious, but other technological problems hampered filmmakers too. Jack Cardiff speaks of changes in equipment and lighting requirements:

When I was photographing Black Narcissus, *the key light on the actor's face had to equal over 1000 candlepower, now we need only 80. In the early days we used white arc-lamps. Then Eastmancolour brought out film which could be used with incandescent light uncorrected. This was a great breakthrough.*

Nowadays, in a dim scene, you can use just one small lamp which you can carry in your hand, without the necessity for covering lights. There was also the nuisance of huge blimps— padded surrounds to render the camera soundproof. In the early days of sound these were like small bungalows—now they are tiny. The BNC Mitchell is in itself a little blimp. All this, together with the smaller cameras, means an enormous increase in freedom for all of us.[7]

Certain filmmakers feel more at home with outdoor settings than with the confines of an indoor location. Satyajit Ray says,

In the exterior settings the details and the light bring essential cinematic ideas. One is in contact with life, which one is not on the stage or studio. The people and the landscape dictate to you elements which have nothing to do with theories, be they even of Eisenstein.[8]

One gains flexibility by preplanning (if possible) as many details as he can in advance. Alfred Hitchcock plans everything except the emotions:

Sometimes I plan as many as six hundred camera set-ups before I begin to shoot. If I ever tried to improvise . . . on the set, I couldn't get the reactions or effects that I want to get.[9]

On the other hand some filmmakers feel that the flexibility is destroyed with too much planning. Richard Lester believes in not scripting camera movements: "I never use a script with any camera directions, simply because I never know what I want before I get on the set."[10] In a third approach, Stanley Kubrick never bothers to think about the camera too soon. "The important thing is not to start thinking of the camera, because you stop concentrating on what's happening and start worrying about how someone will get from one place to another and what will happen to them."[11]

Other filmmakers dislike the technical perfection demanded by today's audiences. Jean Renoir speaks:

All the technical refinements discourage me. Perfect photography, larger screens, hi-fi sounds, all make it possible to enable mediocrities slavishly to reproduce nature, and this reproduction bores me. What interests me is the interpretation of life by an artist.[12]

Technology marches on, despite a discouraging word or two, for the betterment of documentary films and filmmakers. Burden, inconvenience, distraction are the key words in this review of a new camera and film emulsion. Speaking of Kodak's newest high speed film and accompanying camera, Don Sutherland says,

If I could get workable images here, it's easy to envision the same kind of results in the home, under normal room light, the physical burden and inhibiting distraction of movie lights forgotten. . . . It means natural-looking shots can be had without extra paraphernalia and relatively little intrusion. It appears that Kodak's claim is right: the inconvenience of movie lights is obsolete, and the range of things to shoot has expanded tremendously.[13]

So, the documentary filmmaker overcomes the burden of his equipment, concentrates on the events taking place, and records them unobtrusively and naturally. The result? A better documentary, a true view of events: in essence the filmmaker's own way of reacting and communicating with the world around him.

BIBLIOGRAPHY

Butler, Ivan, *The Making of Feature Films (A Guide)*, Middlesex, England, Penguin Books, Ltd., 1971.

Colman, Hila, *Making Movies—Student Films to Features*, New York, World Publishing Company, 1969.

Jacobs, Lewis, *The Movies as Medium*, New York, Doubleday Publishing Company, 1970.

Schickel, Richard, *Movies—The History of an Art and an Institution*, London, MacGibbon and Kee, 1965.

Sutherland, Don, "Super-8 Color for Existing Light," *Popular Photography*, 69:6, December, 1971, p. 141.

[1] Hila Colman, *Making Movies—Student Films to Features*, p. 95.

[2] *Ibid.*, p. 95.

[3] *Ibid.*, p. 96.

[4] *Ibid.*, p. 96f.

[5] *Ibid.*, p. 97.

[6] Richard Schickel, *Movies—The History of an Art Form and an Institution*, p. 115.

[7] Ivan Butler, *The Making of Feature Films* (A Guide), p. 123.

[8] Satyajit Ray, "Film to Film," *Cahiers du Cinema*, No. 3, 1966, quoted in Lewis Jacobs, *The Movies as Medium*, p. 6.

[9] Pete Martin, "Pete Martin Calls on Hitchcock," *Saturday Evening Post*, July, 1967, quoted in Lewis Jacobs, *The Movies As Medium*, p. 6.

[10] "An Interview with Richard Lester," *Saturday Review*, December, 1965, quoted in Lewis Jacobs, *The Movies as Medium*, p. 7.

[11] Stanley Kubrick, "How I Learned to Stop Worrying and Love the Cinema," *Films and Filming*, June, 1963, quoted in Lewis Jacobs, *The Movies as Medium*, p. 6.

[12] Jean Renoir, *Film Book One*, quoted in Lewis Jacobs, *The Movies as Medium*, p. 9.

[13] Don Sutherland, "Super-8 Color by Existing Light," *Popular Photography*, December, 1971, p. 141.

The Effect of the Mode of Interface Between Film-Maker and Event

by Markus John P. Kruesi

BORN: October 14, 1949.

EDUCATION: attended New College, Sarasota, Florida; studied video production and directing at Castleton State College, Castleton, Vermont; attended Columbia College for four semesters as a full-time student; at present on a part-time basis.

EMPLOYMENT: currently employed by Sync-Marc, Inc., as a production manager. Also, I do freelance work. Freelance credits as a soundman include "Old Glory Marching Society," distributed by Perennial Education.

PLANS: become a producer-director. Make films that allow people to laugh.

The mode of interface between the filmmaker and the event does have a definite effect on the film and the subject of the film. Dai Vaughan, in his article entitled "The Man With the Movie Camera," speaks of the importance of the unobtrusiveness. "What matters is that such things" (he is speaking of intimate scenes and behavior) "would not normally be happening *at all* in the accidental presence of cameramen and technicians; and merely to flaunt the presence of the camera gives no clue as to how people might have behaved had the camera not been there." Being unobtrusive is of key importance. The mode of interface, while it is important as a physical determinant of the film, does not necessarily create the desired relationship.

Robert Flaherty has great praise for both the long focal length lens and the small light camera. ". . . it was in filming intimate scenes, and particularly in making portraits, that I learned the true value of long-focus lenses. I began using them to take close-ups in order to obviate self-consciousness on the part of my subjects. The Samoans, I found, acted much more naturally with the camera thirty or forty feet away than when I was cranking right under their noses." This quote comes from the article "Filming Real People" by Flaherty. Flaherty also explains how long focal length lenses permitted him to take shots which he physically could not have gotten otherwise.

Obviously, a silent camera is less noticeable than a noisy one, but silence does not equal being inconspicuous. As Charles Reynolds in his article "Focus On Al Maysles" points out, Maysles seems to have solved the problem of remaining inconspicuous quite well. To quote Al Maysles, "The problem of having people notice the camera is not as big as you might think. If you are overly concerned about the presence of the camera, the people you are filming will be concerned about it, too. The camera stays on my shoulder all the time and sometimes I am shooting with it and sometimes I am not. Since the camera is silent and remains in the same position all day long, they can't tell. If they were to think about the camera all the time, they'd get very tired. It gets to be like part of the furniture in the room." After reading this statement and contrasting it to Flaherty's, I thought about the filmmaker's films. I realized that equipment can enhance the quality of interface but remaining inconspicuous is determined by perceiving the requirements of the subject.

An experience of Robert Edmonds demonstrates this. Filming in a mine, Edmonds realized that miners emerging from an elevator would confront the camera. He made use of the intruder, knowingly. Setting up the big camera, the cameraman filmed, screened by a person with a small Bell & Howell, the lens of which appeared under the armpit of the "screen."

Three different methods accomplishing the same thing: the camera is minimized. The Edmonds example and the point made by Dai Vaughan, that only recently is 16mm sync equipment as light as 35mm silent, made me realize that equipment isn't really the strong point of interface. My realization is small and I don't know how I missed it before, but it has proved useful. Knowing that a friend was to be in a dangerous interview situation, I suggested the use of an additional soundman, both to act as a buffer, in the same way the soundman acts on occasion, in the place of Edmonds' studio camera, and as an object the subject will focus on rather than the taking lens.

Yes, an Eclair is quiet and portable; David Wolper was able to get one into the New York Stock Exchange because he was able to convince the President of the Exchange that it would not cause disruption the way a Hollywood feature crew had done (to such a degree that they had caused a drop in trading). However, that is only the physical side of the question. Mentally, you can stay out of their way, as Flaherty suggests, bore them like Maysles, or, if they're going to stare, give them something else.

All quotations were excerpted from the book *The Documentary Tradition,* edited by Lewis Jacobs.

The Responsibility of the Artist to His Audience

by Keith Davis

Age 24; married; two children.

Education: graduated DuSable High School, January, 1966.
Entered Columbia College, September, 1969; graduating June, 1972.
I entered Columbia in 1969, after having been out of school for three years. While out of school I had been taking music lessons in flute and later on in saxophone at the Chicago Conservatory.

After having dealt with music, I became interested in photography and later enrolled in Columbia where I took some Photo courses.
I studied photography for about a year and then went into motion pictures.

Art has served man in a broad functional way throughout history. Works created by most individuals were generally for the perpetuation of a particular culture, society, group or clan; most expressed the deeds and aspirations of special interest groups. The theory of "art for art's sake," the belief that art results from and serves man as an esthetic non-essential, is a concept of the twentieth century.

The great periods of traditional art in Africa stand as monuments to utilitarian art in that the majority of the works created were made to fulfill the needs of the communities. Because artists worked and created for the benefit of the community making products which belonged to a political milieu and which were marked by general homogeneity, this did not rule out opportunities for individual expression. The African artists, like other artists, express their personal reactions to external stimuli in accordance with the esthetic norms of their community.

The traditional arts of Africa are important in the lives of the people. In Africa, objects that we choose to call art are used in everyday affairs within the community. They are not held in high esteem out of proportion to their service. Should a work be lost or destroyed, a new one is simply made to replace it. This attitude keeps the art alive instead of prolonging the life of an object.

In contrast to African concepts, in the Western world the arts have been traditionally for those in control of power, and they have been used as instruments to maintain and perpetuate their power. Medieval and Renaissance arts of Europe served the church and state and were not without a relationship to sociology. Art was used as an instrument in the glorification of the institutions. During the early periods of church domination, when most people could not read, they learned from "reading" the murals in churches and chapels, state portraits, impressive monumental sculptures, etc. The populace were not only informed but they were impressed with the power and might of those represented by the subject matter. Realizing the medium of control that art provided, both church and state saw to it that the direction of art remained in their hands throughout succeeding centuries. Re-examination of the history of the periods will attest to the fact that art was less of a non-essential esthetic expression and more for political and social control.

Social art was used in the early history of the United States to glorify the actions (any actions) of the government and of those sanctioned by the government. The recording of "heroic" deeds, from crossing the Delaware to killing Indians, was sanctioned and promoted as nationalistic and American. Such art is now prized by museums and regarded as a part of the cultural heritage of this nation.

Any instrument or vehicle may be used for "good" or "bad"; art is no exception. The direction one will take depends upon his particular perspective. In essence the value of an art form or of anything depends to a large extent on the quality of service to a people. If the people only need an art form that provides non-essential esthetics, then that is what should be provided. However, if a people are involved in a revolution and struggle for life, then an added measure of social and political communication would be in order. It all depends on the *place, time,* and *the people.* Only those who are real participants (directly or indirectly) can truly decide. Others may intellectualize on the questions but in matters of life and death (culturally speaking) the participants must decide for themselves.

In following the misdirection implied in the social attitudes in the United States, that art is a luxury item to be used only after we are well fed and our bodies are sheltered, Black people are depriving themselves of a powerful ally in the quest for liberation.

The Function of Topicality in Documentary Films

by Robert Miller

I am a graduate of North Dakota State University with a B.A. in theater. While attending NDSU I served as president of the University Film Society, film critic for the college paper, and program director of the school's educational FM station. I have worked as a writer, announcer, and newsman for commercial radio and television stations since 1963 and hold a degree in broadcast engineering from Radio Engineering Institute in Sarasota, Florida. At the present time I am planning to earn a master's degree in motion pictures, with the hope of making films as an avocation and teaching film history professionally.

Documentary films are generally understood to comprise the body of filmed work taken from life itself. Tome after tome of film criticism repeats their praise of being "real," as distinguished from the "artificial" Hollywood product. Since documentarians have almost universally, and for the most part gladly, accepted this definitive distinction as a starting point for both production and study, this examination of the function of topicality will begin here too.

Speak of life and the word immediately connotes the passage of time—time being so irrevocably intertwined with the problem of existence and accomplishment that life's transient quality has always remained its most observable. One sage tells us to be certain only of death (and taxes), while another admonishes us to be sure only of change itself. Filming from life, therefore, is to wilfully subject one's work to the anchoring aspects of name, place and date—and await the unrelenting onslaught of withering, distorting and distancing time.

A substantial bulwark against the aforementioned hazard, however, is to study and film the parts of life that resist becoming dated, through the process of natural regeneration, either as universal qualities of what we like to call "human nature," or as the continuing ethos and practices of a homogeneous racial, cultural or social group. Here is where one must pay cinematic as well as anthropologic homage to Flaherty. So long as there are non-industrialized Eskimos, South Sea Islanders, men of Aran, or back-country Cajuns, his work will have dated little indeed; when the lives of these people have finally been utterly transformed by the outside world, the Flaherty films will still beautifully portray the primal machinations of man's human nature.

The topical documentarian films from life as well, but by the nature of his approach must forego emphasis on the enduring and universal to provide space in which to grasp the temporal and specific. The life on his screen decays ever so much more quickly, and must be treated with the swiftness and care of a purveyor of prized perishables. A filmmaker undertaking a film on a union dispute in a specific factory or industry cannot help but become equally concerned about finishing and screening his film quickly and the possibility of a quick and beneficial settlement, averting a long and painful strike. To complete his film after the subject has passed from current interest can often mean failure (unless the film is so stunning that it revives interest with bold new insights) and still the concerned filmmaker can find no great joy in seeing a harmful situation continue, despite the fact that it prolongs topical interest and keeps his film in demand. In effect, the topical documentarian with a didactic or reform point of view (which is usually concomitant with most great documentaries) finds himself cast in a role not unlike the physician who abhors and combats disease but would be out of work without it. While the rewards of the topical approach may lie in the chances to further one's ideology, the challenge of time's swift passage can introduce no mean difficulties.

In a larger sense, the passage of time continues to confront us with what John Doremus loved to call the "Passing Parade" of mankind's evolving history. For the better part of this century the filmed record has been of great importance in chronicling and preserving the great and near-great events of civilization. In film libraries and vaults scattered across the world repose the nitrate and acetate images of leaders' speeches, battle scenes, natural disasters, proud ceremonies, and endless mechanical (even artistic) physical creations to amaze, amuse and assist the human family. These, in effect are the raw material of future documentaries of the compilation school. Many of these clips have been used dozens of times in the past to compose documentaries in which the events were no longer topical but the implied meanings of their permutations most certainly were. The effective topicality of compilation documentaries has proven to be almost as elusive as that sought for films made entirely of freshly-shot product. Prime explanation for this phenomenon can be found in what philosophers like to call the transitional Zeitgeist, the ever-changing popular outlook.

This leads us into a most uncomfortable area of investigation, for we are now confronted with the preferably invisible structure and operation of intellectual conformism. Ego-reinforcement has been found to be an emotional nutrient for which we all have a minimum daily requirement, and the most facile means of filling it is to be told that we are right—right in what we do, right in what we say, right in our choice of alternatives (be they food, friends, attire, or amor) and most of all, right in what we think! As new philosophies are tested and accepted by society's vanguard, our secondary (and hence far more numerous) thought leaders are bound together in an unconscious working out of the herd instinct, seeking the approval of their superiors in thinking and doing what has now become right!

What this all means is that a compilation documentary, employing completely genuine footage of actual historical events that are still relevant to contemporary society and the subject of continuing interest, can date—and date badly—with the passage of only a decade or less. The topicality of the film's alignment with what was then the current Zeitgeist is easily lost in the shuffle of changing popular opinions and outlook. An audience viewing such a film, even though the picture may have been a great success with the intellectual population of a few years back, may find that those thoughts that it thinks are, and claims as, its own are not being reinforced by what it is viewing. This *may* then cause the film to be rejected ostensibly on the basis of being incorrect in its interpretation of the events depicted, but since truth is so often obscured by its uncompromisingly relative nature, the film's rejection may really be simply an emotional/visceral reflex response to the denial of ego reinforcement. Nevertheless, the net effect on the film is the deprecatory one of having become dated, due to an unavoidable loss of the proper topicality. Imagine the reception that would await a network screening today of Salomon's NBC documentary, acclaimed in 1955, *Nightmare in Red*.

Present in the heart of many a documentary filmmaker at the outset of making a topical work is, no doubt, the faint glimmer of aspiration that some day his finished work, despite its hazardous topicality, might live on in glory as a film classic. This certainly is no ignoble desire for, as Orson Welles once said, "It's no more immoral to make films for posterity than it is to make films for money"! In light of the restive possibility of filmic immortality, it would be wise to keep in mind one final way to insure one's production against a too-early post-topical death. Such security is by no means easy to come by, and to attain it deliberately is to labor in vain after the fact, for one, it seems, must be born with it. That insuring characteristic of a documentary film destined to be truly great is its aesthetic appeal, the seemingly indefinable qualities of pictorial choice and composition, nuances of tone and presentation, and cohesive success in the whole exceeding the sum of the parts, that can be, and sometimes is, achieved in the work of a genuine film artist. Long after the waters of the Netherlands have subsided, long after the Mississippi has been tamed, long after Timothy has grown to manhood and read his diary to his son, the once-topical documentaries of gifted men such as Ivens, Lorentz and Jennings live on in large part due to what must, for lack of a nobler word, be called simply beauty.

The seeming dichotomy between aesthetic appeal of form and image and expediency of filming illustrated in so many of today's angry documentaries does not appear to have hampered them in the slightest in communicating with ever-increasing audiences. One wonders, in fact, if the overwhelming emphasis on content alone is actually in keeping with the now popular outlook that appearance for its own sake is hypocrisy, and that truth and the unattractive go hand in glove. In Michael Wadleigh's overpowering documentary of rock in the rain and music in the mud, one hears the young enthusiasts repeating, "It's beautiful, man!" to the point where the counterpoint between visual and sound attains a zenith and nadir so distant as to please the most dogmatic of Eisensteinian theoreticians. If contemporary documentary has indeed synthesized a wholly new aesthetic, then it need never fear the fickle passing of the muse of topicality. The mud we will always have with us.

92

Why Can't We Wrap Today's Fish Bones
In Yesterday's Granton Trawler?
or
Whatever Happened To Westbrook Van Voorhis?*

---

by William Utley

Born April 10, 1939, in Aurora, Illinois.

Married; two daughters.

Served in the United States Marine Corps Reserve, 1961-1966.

Education: B.S., Business Administration, Marquette U., 1957-1961.
M.S., Education, Northern Illinois University, 1964-1969.
M.A., Motion Picture Education, Columbia College, Chicago.

Teaching Experience: Fifth and Sixth Grades, Meadowbrook School,
Northbrook, Illinois, 1965-1967.

English, Film Study, Film, Glenbrook South High School, Glenview,
Illinois, 1967-present.

Instructor, Art of the Cinema, History of the Cinema, Columbia
College, Chicago, Illinois, summer semesters, 1970, 1971.

Immediacy. Relevance. Catchwords of our time. In an age
marked by anxious awareness, viewing audiences demand and
devour (rarely disgorge) the fashionable and trendy with seeming delight. Basically, this hyper-awareness has developed as
our mass communications systems gradually put each of us in
almost instantaneous contact with the more remote outskirts
of the "global village" (including our lunar suburb!). We have
become accustomed to daily newscasts from literally everywhere. Television news has taken to topicality—"contemporaneity in reference to allusion"[1]—so overwhelmingly that it has
practically become the newsreel's *raison d'être*. Unfortunately,
the TV newsreel's insistence on the impact of immediacy has
become a Damoclean sword. Since ennui arrives almost as

---

*The high mercury content of the bones eats through the acetate. He is a
part-time voice instructor in the NBC TV news department.

quickly as the news itself, the conditioned expectations of viewers and the passage of time serve as pall bearers and grave digger to the rapidly cooling hot item on yesterday's 6:00 P.M. news.

As we trace back and locate the origins of the television newsreel in the documentary tradition, we can likewise see how topicality has changed, limited, and expanded the effectiveness of various modes of documentary films.

Plainly, the most obvious use of topicality is in terms of subject matter, be it concerned with social, political, or moral issues. In both entertainment and documentary films it has been used to attract audiences. In the early sixties, *Mondo Cane*, a richly photographed, episodic foray into sensationalism, caught the United States by surprise. It quickly became the Inter-"National Enquirer" of documentary films treating its mildly bizarre subjects with the aim of shocking and titillating audiences. It was so wildly successful in its attempt that it quickly became topical itself, generating numerous other pseudo and actual documentaries which tried to cash in on its controversial subject matter. The succeeding string of *ersatz* "Mondos" quickly became tedious, and finally downright tiresome. Today, those of us who bother, remember the film as a quaint, historical oddity.

On the other hand, an exotic, earthy documentary made forty years earlier than *Mondo Cane* is still healthy and full of life. *Nanook of the North* was also a *cause célèbre* of sorts when it opened, startling audiences, becoming topical itself, and inspiring inferior, less successful, imitations. It contains almost as much animal slaughter, unusual eating habits, and nudity as does *Mondo Cane*, yet it is universally recognized as a high watermark, one of the greatest documentary films ever made.

In *Nanook*, the bizarre (to us) episodes are seen in the context of an entire, very human, way of life; in *Mondo Cane* there is a deliberate attempt to wrench the episodes from related contexts, hence a dehumanization of any life which we can catch a glimpse of.

Topicality is employed quite differently in propaganda/political films. Normally, the subject of a documentary film is based upon an issue that is presently, or recently, in the public eye—a subject which, because of its interest and/or possible controversy, will prompt audiences to see the film. However, the main objective of a propaganda film is to promote an idea, person, or political position to an ever-increasing audience—to develop and to *keep* topical whatever the film is about. In *Triumph of The Will* (1934), Leni Riefenstahl was commissioned to extol the virtues and grandeur of Nazism, which, at the time, was by no means acceptable to the majority of Germans. In other words, Hitler was creating a market for his shabby wares. By keeping the message relevant, immediate, he was able to sell a desperate nation a bill of goods. *Olympia* (1937) was a later attempt to gain entry and eventual control of the world "market" with the same "product."

Similarly, Britain's John Grierson used topicality in the documentary movement he founded in the late twenties and guided through the socially disruptive thirties. He has stated that the basic motivation was social, not aesthetic. "We were, I confess, sociologists, a little worried about the way the world was going . . . We were interested in all instruments which would crystallise sentiments in a muddled world and create a will toward civic participation."[2] The film units of the General Post Office and Empire Marketing Board produced hundreds of films on social issues (housing, health, labor, education, politics, etc.) in the interests of good citizenships.[3] The method was to make the subjects of these films topical—to motivate, persuade, and cajole citizen audiences into awareness and appreciation of ordinary British life and its importance in the national fabric.

Of these hundreds of films, a handful remain important today, long after their social concerns have been either solved or forgotten. In spite of their topicality, *Drifters, Granton Trawler, Listen to Britain, Night Mail, Song of Ceylon,* and a few others have transcended their original time, space, and purpose, and speak clearly to us (like *Nanook*) of human beings in a human context.

Our government, as well, produced and distributed hundreds of documentaries for similar topical concerns. In the thirties two outstanding ecological films—*The Plow That Broke the Plains* and *The River*—depicted man's heedless exploitation and destruction of the environment and the government's generally successful attempts to reclaim and reuse those natural resources.

The forties brought national mobilization and world war to the United States. The social concern, public interest, and educational needs of a people at war inspired many kinds of special topic films. From Frank Capra's *Why We Fight* series and John Huston's *Battle of San Pietro* to films on *The M-1 Rifle* and

Your Office of Price Administration, the crucial issues in a muddled world were being crystallized into a unified effort against a common enemy with the help of topical documentary films.[4] Time was crucial, the need for information, instruction, and training great. All the elements of topicality had to be fully exploited, and were in the interests of national survival.

The concern with topicality took a new turn in the fifties and helped to create a new mode of documentary—cinema vérité. Dissatisfaction with the carefully controlled camera set-ups and, in many cases, the rehearsing of the subjects of documentaries, coupled with the development of faster, more sensitive film, smaller cameras, and small, battery-powered tape recorders, and a vague compulsion for more "honest" films, sent film makers scurrying to the streets, literally, in search of "film truth." The urge for immediacy extended beyond its earlier limits of story and theme to include method, as well. The mode now included being witness to contemporary thought and feeling by recording people in the political or social act as it happened—the essence of topicality.

The results of this very topical style of documentary have been a mixed bag of refreshing spontaneity and sheer dullness. Recent national concern and interest in the life styles of the young proved inspirational to the excellent and very profitable film document, *Woodstock*. However, topicality in terms of audience interest in the same subject area and method failed miserably in one of the dimmest (if not dumbest) documentaries released in recent years, the Beatles' *Let It Be*. Yet a National Film Board of Canada documentary, made a few years earlier than *Let It Be,* about a similar social phenomenon, is generally acknowledged as a minor classic.

Lonely Boy, a film about Paul Anka, who was to the pop music public in the late fifties and early sixties what the Beatles later became, makes a devastating, though in parts very lyrical, statement on the question of topicality, its exploitation, and those affected by it. Perhaps it is the ideal example for this essay —a topical film, done in the most topical style, about topicality.

Although its functions vary from film to film, according to purpose, theme, and subject matter, topicality is an important, if limited, element in the documentary tradition. Topicality as an end in itself is deadly. Without thought and attention to aesthetic elements, moral questions, and human insights, a film can be timely; with them it becomes timeless.

[1] *The American Heritage Dictionary.*
[2] Forsyth Hardy, *Grierson on Documentary* (Berkeley: University of California Press, 1966), p. 18.
[3] Lewis Jacobs, "New Trend in British Documentary: Free Cinema," *The Documentary Tradition—From NANOOK to WOODSTOCK*, ed., Lewis Jacobs (New York: Hopkinson and Blake, 1971), p. 338.
[4] Lewis Jacobs, "The Military Experience and After," *Ibid.*, pp. 184-5.

BIBLIOGRAPHY

Hardy, Forsyth, *Grierson on Documentary;* rev. Berkeley: University of California Press, 1966.

Jacobs, Lewis. *The Documentary Tradition—From Nanook to Woodstock.* New York: Hopkinson and Blake, 1971.

Leyda, Jay. *Kino—A History of the Russian and Soviet Film.* London: George Allen & Unwin, Ltd., 1960.

Snyder, Robert L. *Pare Lorentz and the Documentary Film.* Norman: University of Oklahoma Press, 1968.

A Course Outline For Documentary Film
---

by Jeffrey Tassani

I have an Associate of Arts degree from Temple Junior College, Temple, Texas, and a Bachelor of Science degree from the University of Texas at Houston, with a major in radio and television. I spent four and a half years in the service as a captain in the Army, working in instructional television, film, and press relations. I am presently employed at the First National Bank of Chicago as Assistant Vice-President in charge of a group called Media and Communications, which includes television facilities, film facilities, and a graphic artists' group; about 25 people all told.

I am 29 years old, married, and have two children. I live in Buffalo Grove, Illinois.

GOALS

1   To define "Documentary."
2   To familiarize students with the origins of Documentary film.
3   To consider the conditions (historical) that caused or affected the development of Documentaries.
4   To select noteworthy Documentary film producers who illustrate a historical period of Documentary film production for discussion.
5   To be able to clearly distinguish Documentary film ingredients from other types of film.
6   To ensure at the course end that each student has had the opportunity to view many types of Documentary, discuss same, from many different points of view.
7   To relate frequently the topical aspects of Documentary films.
8   To create a conducive atmosphere for loosely structured yet relative discussion.

RATIONALE

I feel that a course in the History of Documentary should be one of the most rewarding and revealing film background courses a student takes.

I have elected to divide the course into five sections, each section covering a decade of documentary film productions. I would furnish the class with a bibliography for reference sources to enable them, if they so elected, to research further each film maker.

If possible I would arrange five guest speakers to talk on each of the five decades concerned. These speakers need not be experts in Documentary but possess a skill or talent that would help fulfill the picture of that decade and how it related to the development of Documentaries.

Early in the course I would distribute a questionnaire to each student to get an idea of the relative level of experience and expertise I was dealing with.

I would divide the class into five groups for the purpose of researching and viewing a decade of documentary film productions. These groups would then lead the discussion and introduce the films of their respective decades. I feel by forcing this type of preparation that the classes would be more meaningful, in that each student would be bringing more to the experience.

I'm hopeful that, inasmuch as the program I have outlined is a fairly structured one, a freedom of meaningful discussion can be realized.

OUTLINE

Section I—The Twenties

Nanook of the North—Robert J. Flaherty
Moana—Robert J. Flaherty
Berlin: The Symphony of a Great City—Walter Ruttman
Rain—Joris Ivens
The Man with the Movie Camera—Dziga Vertov

The following categories should be covered in the discussion:

1   The origin of Documentaries
2   Background of producer

3 Motivation of the times
4 State of the art at that period
5 Budget limitations, if any, at that time
6 Political pressures

Section II—The Thirties

Millions of Us, American Labor Films
The Plow That Broke the Plains, Pare Lorentz
The River, Pare Lorentz
Siege, Julien Bryan
Three Songs About Lenin, Dziga Vertov
Triumph of the Will, Leni Riefenstahl
The following categories should be covered in the discussion:
1 Effects of the Depression
2 Effects of the War
3 National Unity
4 The value of a documentary as a tool of propaganda
5 Comparison of Soviet, German, English and American
   documentaries during this period.

Section III—The Forties

Baptism of Fire, German Army Film
Churchill's Island, Stuart Legg
Fury in the Pacific, U.S. Army, Navy and Marine Corps
The Lion Has Wings, Alexander Korda
Listen to Britain, Humphrey Jennings
London Can Take It, Harry Watt and Humphrey Jennings
Louisiana Story, Robert J. Flaherty
Prelude to War, Frank Capra
The Quiet One, Sidney Meyers

The following categories should be covered in the discussion:
1 Propaganda films in Great Britain and Germany
2 The World situation
3 The War years, before and after
4 Social issues of the day

Section IV—The Fifties

Life Begins Tomorrow, Nicole Vedres
O Dreamland, Lindsay Anderson
On the Bowery, Lionel Rogosin
Salt of the Earth, Herbert J. Biberman
Song of the Rivers, Joris Ivens and Vladimir Pozner
Thursday's Children, Guy Brenton and Lindsay Anderson
The Undefeated, Paul Dickson

The following categories should be covered in the discussion:

1 Korean War effect
2 McCarthyism
3 Cold War
4 Big Business sponsors of documentaries
5 The new money for documentaries
6 Marshall Plan films
7 The effect of television
8 The new freedom in documentary
9 The Atomic Age

Section V—The Sixties

Four Days in November, Mel Stuart
Head Start in Mississippi, Adam Gifford
Law and Order, Frederick Wiseman
Mondo Cane, Gualtiero Jacopetti
Morley Safer's Vietnam
No Vietnamese Ever Called Me Nigger, David Loeb Weiss
The Olive Trees of Justice, James Blue
Primary, Richard Leacock, Robert Drew, D. A. Pennebaker,
          and Albert Maysles
The Tenement, Jay McMullen

The following categories should be covered in the discussion:

1 Integration
2 The Vietnam War
3 Pollution
4 Campus Unrest

5 Assassinations

6 Cinéma-Vérité

7 The economy

EVALUATION (Exam)

Each student will be required to write a paper of general information about a section (decade) of Documentary Film Production. In each paper, the following list of points should be covered and expanded on for that time period:

1 Definition of Documentary.

2 A consideration of the historical conditions that caused or affected the development of documentary to the state of the art for that period.

3 To include a discussion of the noteworthy documentary films and filmmakers of that period.

4 To relate as frequently as possible to the topical aspects for that period.

In conjunction with the paper outlined above, each student would make a 15 minute presentation. As I indicated in the Rationale, the class would be divided into five groups, each group selecting the films for their specific period. Each student would make a 15 minute presentation on a different aspect of his documentary period, so ideally every student would hear five different topics on each documentary film period. These presentations coupled with the films and guest speakers would provide a fair standard of achievement in documentary films.

FILMS AND SOCIAL ISSUES

A Course on Documentary Films
for the High School
by May Pietz

I am presently teaching three film courses at Niles North High School
in Skokie, Illinois. Although I sampled other careers early in my
working life, including dancing and flying airplanes, I have been
professionally interested in education for over fifteen years. This
includes teaching nursery school, primary grades, junior high and
college. Currently I am short film editor for SEE magazine, a publication for film teachers.

QUESTIONS I HAVE RAISED
ON TEACHING HIGH SCHOOL FILM COURSES

What kind of film courses suit the high school age?

What specialized film study course would suit students who
have had a basic course in the elements of film?

How can filmmaking be taught to students who have no
experience in making films but would like to make a film as a
form of report in a class not centered on film production?

How can students' concerns for social issues and their
solutions be incorporated into a course for high school?

How can a film course develop sensitivity to film forms
beyond the popular entertainment film?

How can a film course increase the students' personal skills
in judging films?

How can a film course engage student interest beyond
responding to films through discussion and writing?

QUESTIONS I HAVE ASKED
ON DOCUMENTARY FILMS

What is a documentary film?

What forms do documentary films have?

Are there any limits to the form a documentary can take
and still be a documentary?

What differences are there between a television documentary
and an independently-produced documentary film?

Why is the documentary form difficult for students to
appreciate if not enjoy?

Which particular documentary films engage rather than turn
off most general audiences?

What is the present state of the documentary in relation to
the prognosis of the 30s, 40s, and 50s that it was the powerful,
hopeful and dynamic form of cinema?

What areas of social issues are being filmed and which
ones are not? Why?

How does film present, distort or "create" truths?

What is truth?

What is the difference between passionate commitment and
propaganda? Is propaganda good or bad?

How does a person judge real rather than reconstructed
documentaries? Can the viewer tell the difference?

How do films manipulate reality and what is the filmmaker's
responsibility to himself, his subject and his audience?

If truth is subjective, what restrictions or criteria are valid in
presenting a cinematic truth in a documentary film?

Which filmmakers are making significant, effective and
personally committed films?

What are the consequences of our current involvement
in craftsmanship and technology, particularly video-tape,
computers and cybernetics?

How do the mass media affect the personal and aesthetic
shaping of a film?

ONE ANSWER: FILMS AND SOCIAL ISSUES
a course in documentary films for high school

I. COURSE DESCRIPTION

FILMS AND SOCIAL ISSUES is a course for high school students who have previously studied film as a medium but who do not necessarily have any training in the making of films. The course organizes a study of social issues through films and a study of films through an examination of content, viewpoint, form, style and exhibition of a major area of documentary films —those concerned with significant, contemporary social issues.

The exploration of films for understanding social issues links the students' need for information, appreciation and commitment to social problems with the medium which is most suitable for communicating both the evidence and the guts of any issue —the medium of film. To provide a direct experience in observing, recording and formulating a presentation on an issue of importance to any student, each one will work in a small group to produce a short, simple documentary film. So that this film succeeds as both a documentary film and an expression of the students' ideas about the problem they have chosen, the course will include a mini-project on the use of a simple camera and a tape recorder. A team of interested professionals, skilled students and the classroom teacher will conduct the mini-project.

The students will view and respond to films on social issues ranging from television specials to independently-made films in documentary or cinema-vérité style. The emphasis on contemporary issues will exclude older documentaries except when they are necessary to elucidate style, technique or the concept of subjectivity-objectivity.

II. RATIONALE FOR THE COURSE

This course is a confluence of personal experiences and ideas emerging from the teaching of film study and filmmaking in junior and senior high school. The following list of concepts and observations is the foundation for the development of the course:

1   All students see films but not all students are interested in films per se, in spite of the many hours they spend watching films on TV and attending commercial movies.

2 Some students are particularly interested in the vital social concerns of today, to the extent of walking miles to draw attention to poverty, traveling to Washington for war protests, working with handicapped children, assisting in day-care centers or tutoring programs, or actively participating in programs designed to help others or to extend beyond their own personal problems.

3 Students' concepts of documentaries is frequently limiting, even dangerous, to them. Their concept of objectivity-subjectivity is often naïve, restricted to the myth of two-sides-to-an-argument and formed greatly by the pervasive, conservative influence of television.

4 By nature of their adolescence they are frequently imbalanced in their emotional commitment or resistance to social issues.

5 Their appreciation of films extends only slightly beyond entertainment or escapist cinema, including, perhaps, *Woodstock* or *Gimme Shelter*, but for the most part not to documentary films.

6 High school students exaggerate but exemplify a natural interest in current events and for them the past acquires meaning when it is clearly related to the here and now.

7 Our highly technical, electronic, cybernetic society attracts young people without automatically providing any essential education in assessing its nature, so that participation in such a society may lack awareness and judgment about the nature of technical progress.

8 In a broad sense, emotion is suspect in the American culture. This complex, national characteristic affects the teenager in a variety of ways, both culturally and personally, extending to the attitude that a scientific, impersonal statement implies a greater intellectual achievement and social benefit than a passionate, personal statement in any of the informational media.

9 Our national notion of facts, reality and truth as they are expressed through the communication arts is as confused as our personal ones expressed through our responses to these arts. Traditionally students associate documentaries with information or instruction and often boredom. That these films can engage their interest in either the viewing or the making is an uncommon but fruitful idea.

III. OBJECTIVES

TO EXTEND the students' interest in social issues through contemporary, documentary films.

TO EXPAND the students' understanding of film through viewing films, responding to films and making their own documentary film.

TO EXPLODE the myth that there is an objective documentary presentation of any subject.

TO ENCOURAGE subjectivity in the making of a student documentary as a necessity in making a personal commitment in relation to a significant and controversial issue.

TO EXPLORE the degrees of subjectivity in documentaries and the forms, styles and techniques used to editorialize.

TO EXCITE the student about the possibilities of film-as-propaganda for positive and not necessarily evil purposes.

TO EXAMINE the way filmmakers manipulate time, space and reality and the way that external influences—financial, censorial, professional, cultural, etc.—manipulate the filmmakers.

IV. FILMS ON SOCIAL ISSUES

"Entertainment, amusement or recreational cinema has its place in society but not as the totality of cinematic production. Propaganda, education or documentary are essential in society because they concern themselves with the flesh-and-blood, real people and events, and because of their form have the potential for regenerating society." ". . . with its powers to enlarge the public's social conscience, to create new standards of culture, to stir mental apathies, and by virtues inherent in its form, to become the most powerful of all modern preachers, it is absurd to suggest it can be left in the hands of commercial speculators to be used as a vehicle for purposeless, fictional stories."[1]

The broadest definition of documentary films might be nonfictional films. Grierson's brief description is "the creative treatment of actuality."[2] The definition that more precisely distinguishes a documentary is a film about . . ."real people and real events, indigenous to its time, in which man is shown in relationship to other men, to his job or to his environment in an artistically selected and arranged manner to express truth."[3]

Further limiting documentaries to films on social issues for this course recognizes the subjective nature of classification as well as of truth.

The film selections are based more on personal considerations than on a formalized set of criteria. I have chosen films that I feel will appeal strongly to teenagers on the basis of style, subject or topicality. Other choices consider the young person's strong interest in self-understanding or personal competence. The documentary's focus on reality and truth suggests films that deal honestly with basic human issues of such significance that they are most likely controversial. My responsibility to my students and to myself includes a continuous extension of my awareness, in this case, social awareness, so that films which expand social consciousness and extend perceptions on social issues are vital. The excellent documentaries about the war in Vietnam and the burgeoning concern about this war make it one of the obligatory issues.

The impact of television and its role in providing a forum and capturing an audience for documentaries makes this a productive resource. Further, this form of documentary has developed the talents of some of the most interesting, contemporary, documentary filmmakers. Students seem least critical in their response to television relative to films. The whole spectrum of reportage, information, facts, propaganda, objectivity, subjectivity and censorship is integrated into the study of television documentaries. Television production provides an interesting contrast to the whole field of independent film production.

V. THE DOCUMENTARY FILM AS ART

The duality of the course has virtues: social issues are approached through the attractive medium of film and the study of the medium of film, which is a complex art, is reduced to a manageable range of subjects and forms. One danger of studying both film and society is that the two interests have such a magnetic strength that this duality interferes with the student's sense of direction and satisfaction. The fusion should be one in which the emphasis is on the social issues with a natural, corresponding interest in the filmmaker's attitude toward his subject. This links the question of what is told with how it is told. The appreciation of the elements of film art through a documentary is distinct from art-for-art's-sake and integrates art with its function in society—to bring us the observations and interpretations of the person who is skilled in perceiving, feeling, thinking and expressing what he perceives, feels and thinks through art forms, in this case, film. If art becomes isolated from the ". . . living scene and the living theme, springing from the living present . . . , it becomes the possession of the wealthy, art for art's sake, symbolic, abstract or mystical and therefore removed from the understandings and needs of society in general."[4]

The more specific goal of appreciating film as art is to encourage responses to documentary films which are exciting because they present reality rather than fiction. This is possible, but not easy, because the technical limitations, shooting restrictions, demands of real time and space contrast sharply with the slick commercials and professional conventions of theatrical films. "Real and creative thought must be about real things. Let cinema explore outside the limits of what we are told constitutes entertainment. . . . If it is to mean anything, if it is to survive, a film must have a purpose beyond itself. In the past, cinema has served profit-making motives because it is a fabulously expensive art, thus depriving the artist of his theme. The advancement in technology has occupied technicians with experiments for their own sake, thus developing brilliant craftsmanship with little contribution to modern society. The major works of art in any time are those deeply rooted in and serving those times, and their historical virtues or contributions to later societies were incidental, based on universal understanding of human values significant to any age."[5]

Far from being a stepchild in the art world, the documentary has great aesthetic potential going beyond ". . . the simple descriptive terms of the teaching film, more imaginative and expressive than the specific publicity picture, deeper in meaning and more skillful in style than the newsreel, wider in observation than the travel picture and lecture film, more profound in implication and reference than the plain interest picture."[6] The concern in any film course for developing aesthetic sensibilities is both philosophical and practical. Art is essential to any society. Students are unconsciously, as well as consciously, sensitive to the influences of art whether this is a part of the home, the school or the community environment. They enjoy paintings or posters on the surfaces of their habitats, colors that cheer and interest them, textures that please their hands, feet or eyes, sculptures or objects that move or satisfy the touch and sounds that excite, intrigue or soothe. The documentary as art relates to this role of art in ordinary living. It is a form that appeals because of its sense of reality and credibility. It is reality organized and altered artistically and is therefore interesting to young people just as their music, posters and free-wheeling clothes are interesting to them.

VI. COURSE OUTLINE

Documentaries whose subjects may be classified as social issues permit a flexible organization in relation to particular students and contemporary events. Some of the current and continuing issues are education, the role of women, the changing state and status of blacks in American society, war, community problems and personal problems. Choices of television documentaries is a separate concern: subject matter covers a range of issues but the documentaries belong in one unit so that the matter of style, financing, censorship and the nature of mass media can be integrated with the documentaries. Another area of study might be the documentaries of one or more young, independent documentary filmmakers.

Suggested outline:

A A PREVIEW: three films that captivate young audiences and suggest a great deal about the entire course, including the intrusion of the camera upon the event itself.
The Sixties
Television Land
Shadows and Reflections

B EDUCATION: an examination of the environment we are in right now as students and the question of truth which can be explored within the film class, the school and the films themselves.
Sixteen In Webster Groves
Webster Groves Revisited
High School
Summerhill
Bright College Years
Thursday's Children

C   WAR: a direct look at the war in Vietnam from a variety of viewpoints, with films by French, British and American film-makers.
Basic Training
War Game
Interviews With My Lai Veterans
Anderson Platoon
Seventeenth Parallel
In the Year of the Pig
Once Upon a War
No Vietnamese Ever Called Me Nigger

D   COMMUNITY PROBLEMS: an extension beyond the immediate and personal to some real concerns in films that get to the heart of the matter:
Hospital
Law and Order
Warrendale
Gimme Shelter

E   MEN AND WOMEN: verifying the growing interest in women's lib through exploring roles of men and women in our society, including black men and women.
Lonely Boy
Salesman
Radcliffe Blues
An Actor Works
The Queen
To Be a Man
Interview with Bruce Gordon
Bushman
This Is the Home of Mrs. Levant Graham

F   TELEVISION DOCUMENTARIES: analyzing a particular form of documentary while viewing television documentary films on social issues.
The Selling of the Pentagon
Chiefs
Black Natchez
The Battle of East St. Louis

G   INDEPENDENT DOCUMENTARY FILMMAKERS: the selections for the foregoing units include films by some of the best known and most lively filmmakers—Ed Pincus, Albert

and David Maysles, Arthur Barron, Richard Leacock, Donn
Pennebaker, Frederick Wiseman and Lindsey Anderson.
The choice for this unit, however, might be a local documentary
filmmaker such as Gordon Temaner, Jerry Quinn or Tom
Palazzolo. The filmmakers might come to school and partici-
pate in the discussions about their films.
The Bride Stripped Bare
The Pigeon Lady
Marco
Home for Life

VII. READINGS

Levin, G. Roy. *Documentary Explorations*. Doubleday, 1971.

Jacobs, Lewis. *The Documentary Tradition*. Hopkinson and
Blake, 1971.

These two recent paperback books should appeal to students
and provide them with background, personal data and interesting information about documentary films. The Levin book is a
collection of interviews that reveal personalities, problems and
approaches to documentary filmmaking, controversies and
criticisms that give excitement and possibly new meanings
beyond the experience of the films themselves. There is so much
of interest about the individual filmmaker in each interview
that the usual difficulty with film books—that you haven't seen
all the films talked about—is far less important. Jacobs' book
is an excellent second source, a fine anthology that refers to
some of the most remarkable of documentary films and includes some of the best writings about these films. Although
it is basically an historical organization of material, the last
hundred or more pages deal with a variety of writings about
contemporary documentary films and filmmakers. The bibliography about the subjects of the films in the course would
ideally be compiled at the time of the course and include
periodicals, newspapers and books in the area of film as well
as social issues.

112

NOTES

[1] *Documentary Film.* Paul Rotha. London: Faber and Faber, 1952, p. 105.

[2] *Ibid.,* p. 69, (quoted from John Grierson).

[3] A definition formulated by Robert Edmonds, Chairman of the Motion Picture Department of Columbia College, Chicago.

[4] Rotha. op. cit., p. 65.

[5] *Ibid.,* p. 65.

[6] *Ibid.,* p. 67.

BIBLIOGRAPHY

Rotha, Paul. *Documentary Film.* London: Faber and Faber, 1971.

Levin, G. Roy. *Documentary Explorations.* Garden City, N.Y.: Doubleday and Co., Inc., 1971.

Jacobs, Lewis. *The Documentary Tradition.* New York: Hopkinson and Blake, 1971.

Bluem, A. William. *Documentary in American Television.* New York: Hastings House, 1965.

Hardy, Forsyth, editor. *Grierson on Documentary.* Berkeley: University of California Press, 1966.

Pietz, May. *See.* "Short Films in Review: Documentaries." Chicago: Film Education Resources Corporation, p. 16. (November, 1971)

APPENDIX A

The films named in Introduction, Chapter VIII, are listed more accurately below together with the names of their filmmakers.

Title	Filmmakers
Moscow Clad in Snow	Pathé Frères
Man With a Movie Camera	Dziga Vertov
Rain	Joris Ivens
Granton Trawler	Edgar Anstey (produced and photographed by John Grierson)
Nanook of the North	Robert Flaherty
Berlin, Symphony of a Great City	Walter Ruttman
Gamla Sta'n	Stig Almqvist
New Earth	Joris Ivens
The River	Pare Lorentz
Grass	Ernest B. Schoedsack and Merian C. Cooper
Moana	Robert Flaherty
Le Tempestaire	Jean Epstein
Le Mistral	Joris Ivens
Bambini in Cittá	Luigi Commencini
Thursday's Children	Guy Benton and Lindsay Anderson
A Child Went Forth	John Ferno and Joseph Losey
Children Adrift	Edouard Luntz
My Own Yard to Play In	Phil Lerner
In the Street	Helen Levitt, Janice Loeb and James Agee
Housing Problems	Arthur Elton and Edgar Anstey
Enough to Eat	Edgar Anstey
Land Without Bread	Luis Buñuel
Dead Birds	Robert Gardner
Beaver Country	John J. Carey
Louisiana Story	Robert Flaherty
Turksib	Victor Turin
Report From China	Toshie Tokieda
Le Retour	Henri Cartier-Bresson and Richard Banks
Night and Fog	Alain Resnais
Battle of Algiers	Gillo Pontecorvo

APPENDIX B

The films listed in Films and Social Issues, Chapter VIII, are set forth here together with the names of their filmmakers or producing organizations.

A PREVIEW

The Sixties	Charles Braverman
Television Land	Charles Braverman
Shadows and Reflections	Seth Hill

EDUCATION

Sixteen In Webster Groves	Arthur Barron (CBS News)
Webster Groves Revisited	Arthur Barron (CBS News)
High School	Frederick Wiseman
Summerhill	National Film Board of Canada
Bright College Years	Peter Rosen
Thursday's Children	Guy Benton and Lindsay Anderson

WAR

Basic Training	Frederick Wiseman
War Game	Peter Watkins
Interviews With My Lai Veterans	Joseph Strick
Anderson Platoon	Pierre Schoendorffer (ORTF)
*Seventeenth Parallel	Joris Ivens
In the Year of the Pig	Emile de Antonio
Once Upon a War	Patricia Penn (American Friends Service Committee)
No Vietnamese Ever Called Me Nigger	David Loeb Weiss

COMMUNITY PROBLEMS

Hospital	Frederick Wiseman
Law and Order	Frederick Wiseman
Warrendale	Allan King
Gimme Shelter	Albert and David Maysles

MEN AND WOMEN

Lonely Boy	National Film Board of Canada
Salesman	Albert and David Maysles
Radcliffe Blues	Claudia Weill and Tony Granz
An Actor Works: A scene from	
The Trojan Women	Doubleday Media Inc.
The Queen	Frank Simon
To Be a Man	Murray Lerner
Interview with Bruce Gordon	Harold Becker
Bushman	David Schikele
This Is the Home of Mrs. Levant	
Graham	Claudia Weill and Elliot Noyes

TELEVISION DOCUMENTARIES

The Selling of the Pentagon	CBS News
Chiefs	Richard Leacock
Black Natchez	Ed Pincus and David Neuman
The Battle of East St. Louis	Peter Wolff

INDEPENDENT DOCUMENTARY FILMMAKERS

The Bride Stripped Bare	Tom Palazzolo
The Pigeon Lady	Tom Palazzolo
Marco	Gordon Quinn and Gerald Temaner
Home for Life	Gordon Quinn and Gerald Temaner

*This may also be listed as *17th Parallel*.